General James Longstreet in the West

A Monumental Failure

CIVIL WAR CAMPAIGNS AND COMMANDERS SERIES

Under the General Editorship of Grady McWhiney

PUBLISHED

Battle in the Wilderness: Grant Meets Lee by Grady McWhiney
Death in September: The Antietam Campaign
        by Perry D. Jamieson
Texans in the Confederate Cavalry by Anne J. Bailey
Sam Bell Maxey and the Confederate Indians by John C. Waugh
The Saltville Massacre by Thomas D. Mays
General James Longstreet in the West: A Monumental Failure
        by Judith Lee Hallock
The Battle of the Crater by Jeff Kinard

FORTHCOMING

Cottonclads! The Battle of Galveston and the Defense of the
        Texas Coast by Donald S. Frazier
A Deep, Steady Thunder: The Battle of Chickamauga
        by Steven E. Woodworth
The Texas Overland Expedition by Richard Lowe
Raphael Semmes and the Alabama by Spencer C. Tucker

General James Longstreet in the West
A Monumental Failure

Judith Lee Hallock

Under the General Editorship of Grady McWhiney

McWHINEY
FOUNDATION
PRESS

McMURRY UNIVERSITY
ABILENE, TEXAS

Cataloging-in-Publication Data

Hallock, Judith Lee, 1940—
    General James Longstreet in the West: a monumental failure/
Judith Lee Hallock.
        p. cm. — (Civil War campaigns and commanders)
    Includes bibliographical references and index.
    ISBN 1-886661-04-9

    1. Longstreet, James, 1821–1904. 2. Tennessee—History—
Civil War, 1861–1865—Campaigns. 3. United States—History—Civil
War, 1861–1865—Campaigns. I. Title. II. Series.
    E476.1.L55H35 1995
    973.7'37—dc20   95–33504
                                                              CIP

All inquiries regarding volume purchases of this book should be addressed to
McWhiney Foundation Press, McMurry Station, Box 637, Abilene, TX 79697-0637.
Telephone inquiries may be made by calling (915) 691-6681.

A Note on the Series

Few segments of America's past excite more interest than
Civil War battles and leaders. This ongoing series of brief,
lively, and authoritative books–*Civil War Campaigns and
Commanders*–salutes this passion with inexpensive and
accurate accounts that are readable in a sitting. Each volume,
separate and complete in itself, nevertheless conveys the
agony, glory, death, and wreckage that defined America's
greatest tragedy.

In this series, designed for Civil War enthusiasts as well as
the newly recruited, emphasis is on telling good stories.
Photographs and biographical sketches enhance the narrative
of each book, and maps depict events as they happened. Sound
history is meshed with the dramatic in a format that is just
lengthy enough to inform and yet satisfy.

Grady McWhiney
General Editor

CONTENTS

Introduction   13

1. In the East   17

2. Chickamauga   25

3. Chattanooga   38

4. Wauhatchie   54

5. Knoxville   69

6. Conclusion   81

Appendix A. Organization of Federal Forces   86

Appendix B. Organization of Confederate Forces   104

Further Reading   126

Index   129

CAMPAIGNS AND COMMANDERS SERIES

Map Key

Geography

	Trees
	Marsh
	Fields
	Strategic Elevations
	Rivers
	Tactical Elevations
	Fords
	Orchards
	Political Boundaries

Human Construction

	Bridges
	Railroads
	Tactical Towns
	Strategic Towns
	Buildings
	Church
	Roads

Military

	Union Infantry
	Confederate Infantry
	Cavalry
	Artillery
	Headquarters
	Encampments
	Fortifications
	Permanant Works
	Hasty Works
	Obstructions
	Engagements
	Warships
	Gunboats
	Casemate Ironclad
	Monitor
	Tactical Movements
	Strategic Movements

*Maps by
Donald S. Frazier, Ph.D.
Abilene, Texas*

MAPS

Longstreet's Route to Georgia 26

Northwest Georgia 27

Chickamauga, September 20, 1863 29

Longstreet's Plan of Attack 30

Longstreet's Breakthrough 31

Horseshoe Ridge 33

Chattanooga 39

Lookout Mountain 55

Brown's Ferry, October 27, 1863 59

Wauhatchie, October 28, 1863 64

Longstreet's East Tennessee Campaign 72

Campbell's Station, November 16, 1863 73

Knoxville 74

Fort Sanders 75

Attack on Fort Sanders, November 29, 1863 79

PHOTOGRAPHS

James Longstreet	18
Jefferson Davis	19
Braxton Bragg	20
Robert E. Lee	22
Leonidas Polk	28
Arthur M. Manigault	32
Daniel Harvey Hill	42
Simon Bolivar Buckner	44
Patrick R. Cleburne	46
William Preston	47
William W. Mackall	48
Lafayette McLaws	49
Louis T. Wigfall	50
James A. Seddon	52
George H. Thomas	56
Ulysses S. Grant	58
Micah Jenkins	60
Evander McIvor Law	62
G. Moxley Sorrel	65
Edward Porter Alexander	66
Ambrose Everett Burnside	70
Fort Sanders	76-77
Title page of *A Diary from Dixie*	82

The brief biographies accompanying the photographs were written by
Grady McWhiney and David Coffey.

General James Longstreet in the West

A Monumental Failure

Introduction

The Fourth of July—the day Americans had celebrated their independence for nearly nine decades—was a disastrous day for the Confederate States of America. Three ongoing campaigns culminated on that day in 1863, each catastrophic to the Southern cause.

In the East, General Robert E. Lee's attempt to invade the North, drawing troops away from Virginia for the crop-growing season, ended at Gettysburg, Pennsylvania, during the first three days of July. On the Fourth, Lee began his retreat from the bloody fields.

In the West (the area between the Appalachian Mountains and the Mississippi River) the Federals planned to carry out their Anaconda Plan which would split the South in two by pushing down the Mississippi to the Gulf of Mexico and then slowly squeezing the Confederacy to death between the Union's Western and Eastern armies. Here the Southerners suffered two blows. On the Fourth of July, after a six-week siege, Vicksburg, the last major Confederate defense along the Mississippi, fell to General Ulysses S. Grant, giving the

Federals access to the entire length of the great waterway, splitting the Confederacy in two. The second blow proved equally calamitous.

In the fall of 1862, General Braxton Bragg had invaded Kentucky with the expectation that under the protection of Southern troops, the neutral state would declare for the Confederacy. The campaign failed, and Bragg settled down in Tullahoma, Tennessee, for the winter. However, in late December the Federal army, under General William S. Rosecrans, advanced from Nashville for the purpose of securing the supply lines that ran into the city, thus eliminating any threats from the Confederates for the coming winter. To accomplish this, the Federals had to occupy Murfreesboro, Tennessee. Rosecrans's move forced Bragg into battle on December 31, 1862, and January 2, 1863. Soundly thrashed, Bragg spent that winter and spring at Tullahoma, keeping a wary eye on the Federals poised just miles away at Murfreesboro.

Rosecrans declined to advance until late June, but when he did he quickly routed Bragg's Army of Tennessee. Bragg withdrew southward eighty-five miles and did not stop until he had crossed the Tennessee River and reached Chattanooga, an important railroad center, on the Fourth of July 1863.

Bragg's retreat cost the Confederacy all of Middle Tennessee, an area rich in agricultural products, livestock, iron and other raw materials essential to the war effort, and manpower.

For nearly two months following the Tullahoma Campaign, Rosecrans bided his time, repairing the railroad, gathering supplies, and preparing his army for an advance. In late August he began his push to the south, sending three columns on widely-separated routes through the mountainous region around Chattanooga.

In an effort to forestall a flanking movement that would sever his line of communications and supply, Bragg ordered his army out of Chattanooga. Moving generally southward, the Confederate Army missed splendid opportunities to defeat the widely-dispersed Federals. These failures are directly attributable to Bragg's subordinates, particularly generals Thomas C. Hindman and Leonidas Polk, whose refusals to obey orders twice allowed the Northerners to escape unscathed from precarious positions. Polk, an Episcopal bishop as well as a general, had been a thorn in the western theater from the beginning of the war. He refused to follow the most basic orders, instead following his own inclinations. He never accepted responsibility for the catastrophes his actions incurred; rather, he blamed others, usually his commanding officer. Polk's presence in the Army of Tennessee caused great disaffection among the upper echelons of the officer corps, and much grief to General Bragg.

After retreating southward for several days, Bragg turned north, intending to interpose his army between Rosecrans and Chattanooga while still protecting his own lines of communications. The two enemies met along the banks of Chickamauga Creek, a Native American name meaning "River of Death," on September 18, skirmishing and jockeying for position in preparation for the coming battle.

Bragg, believing his army's right wing outflanked the Federals, planned to drive the enemy southward into McLemore's Cove, where they could be trapped and destroyed. During the night, however, Rosecrans extended his line, and the battle on the nineteenth became one of uncoordinated fighting all along the front. As the battle progressed, Bragg shifted troops from the left to the right, hoping to gain the upper hand and begin the planned roll-up of the Federal Army. Night fell before either side achieved a decided advantage.

There had been much confusion among the Army of Tennessee during the day's battle. Polk, who had started the day commanding the Confederate left, ended the day in command of the right. The commander of the left wing on the second day of battle would be a newcomer to the Western army. He arrived in the middle of the night with about half of his soldiers. They had spent several days traveling from Virginia. The authorities in Richmond, long considering the reinforcement of Bragg's army with Eastern troops, typically delayed reaching a decision until all was nearly lost. As one of Bragg's staffers commented, "They come after the damage has been done, a lock and key on the stable door after the horse has been stolen—such has been the action of Jeff Davis in the Western Campaign, always too late."

Not only too late, but the wrong man for the position. When General James Longstreet arrived in the West, he brought with him the seeds of further disasters to the Confederate cause.

1
IN THE EAST

On September 19, 1863, a train rumbled its way toward Catoosa Station, Georgia. Aboard rode forty-two-year-old Lieutenant General James Longstreet with a heart full of ambition and hope. He believed that he carried within himself the ability to vanquish the Union armies in the West, a feat that would surely win for his beloved Confederacy the independence it so earnestly sought. "My own desire in the matter is to save the country," he had written to a fervent supporter in the Confederate Congress. "I hope that I may get west in time to save what there is left of us." Sadly, he did not possess the ability to accomplish what he expected, and his ambition to command the Army of Tennessee would not be satisfied.

Longstreet, a native of Georgia, had transplanted himself to Alabama in order to obtain an appointment to the United States Military Academy at West Point in the class of 1842. Upon graduation, he ranked a poor fifty-fourth in a field of fifty-six. During the antebellum years Longstreet served in the Mexican War and on the Western frontier.

In 1848 he married Maria Louisa Garland, who would be his loyal supporter. The couple had ten children, only five of whom survived childhood. In January 1862, three of their children died in one dreadful week.

James Longstreet: born South Carolina 1821; graduated U.S. Military Academy fifty-fourth in his class in 1842; appointed a brevet 2d lieutenant in the 4th Infantry the same year; promoted to 2d lieutenant in the 8th Infantry in 1845, and to 1st lieutenant in 1847; won brevet promotions to captain and major for gallant conduct in the battles of Contreras, Churubusco, and Molino del Rey during the Mexican War; served as regimental adjutant from 1847 to 1849; promoted to captain in 1852 and to major

(paymaster department) in 1858; appointed Confederate brigadier general, served at First Manassas, and promoted to major general in 1861; distinguished service during Peninsular Campaign, Second Manassas, Sharpsburg, and Fredericksburg in 1862; promoted to lieutenant general in 1862, "Old Pete" became General Lee's senior corps commander; on detached service south of the James River in May 1863 thus missing the action at Chancellorsville; commanded right wing of Lee's army at Gettysburg in July 1863; took his corps by rail to Chickamauga, Georgia, in September 1863 to help defeat General William S. Rosecrans, but failed in his attempt to capture Knoxville, Tennessee; returned to Virginia in 1864 in time to participate in the Battle of the Wilderness, where he sustained a critical wound that incapacitated him until late fall; led his corps during closing months of the war in defense of Richmond; surrendered with Lee to Grant at Appomattox Court House; after the war, he settled in New Orleans, became a Republican, and as a state militia officer led black troops against Confederate veterans during Reconstruction disturbances; enjoyed political patronage from Republicans; wrote his war memoirs, *From Manassas to Appomattox*; died at Gainesville, Georgia, in 1904. Lee called Longstreet "my old War Horse." An able battlefield tactician, he was at times stubborn, quarrelsome, and overconfident in his ability as an independent commander.

Although Longstreet did not see fit to resign his position as a U.S. Army officer until May 9, 1861, already in February he offered his military services to the state of Alabama and received appointment as brigadier general in the Confederate Army on July 1. Until he joined Bragg at Chickamauga all of Longstreet's Civil War experience had been in the East, where

Jefferson Davis: born Kentucky 1808; attended Transylvania University; graduated U.S. Military Academy twenty-third in his class in 1828; appointed 2d lieutenant in the 1st Infantry in 1828; 1st lieutenant 1st Dragoons 1833; regimental adjutant 1833 to 1834; served on the Northwest frontier and in the Black Hawk War in 1832; resigned from the army in 1835 and eloped with Zachary Taylor's daughter, who died of malaria three months after their marriage; Davis settled in Mississippi as a planter; married Varina Howell and elected to Congress in 1845; resigned to participate in the Mexican War; appointed colonel 1st Mississippi Volunteer Infantry in 1846; serving under Taylor, he was wounded at Buena Vista in 1847; declined appointment to brigadier general; elected senator from Mississippi in 1847; secretary of war under President Franklin Pierce from 1853 to 1857; returned to the Senate where he served on military affairs committee until his resignation in 1861; president of the Confederate States of America from 1861 to 1865; captured following the war in Georgia, he was imprisoned at Fort Monroe for two years and never brought to trial; after failing in a number of business ventures, he was a poor man  during his later years, living at "Beauvoir," a house on the Gulf of Mexico given to him by an admirer; Mississippi would have sent him to the Senate, but he refused to ask for the Federal pardon without which it was impossible for him to take his seat; published *The Rise and Fall of the Confederate Government* in 1881; died in New Orleans in 1889. A biographer called Davis "a very engaging young man, fearless, generous, modest, with personal charm, and in friendship rashly loyal." His loyalty to the Southern cause also never faltered. But as a president he proved to be prideful, stiff, stubborn, often narrow-minded, unwilling to compromise. These qualities kept him from becoming a great chief executive.

he had become one of General Lee's closest associates. Promoted to lieutenant general on October 9, 1862, Longstreet held an independent command in the Department of Virginia and North Carolina from February to April 1863, after which he rejoined Lee for the Gettysburg Campaign.

Powerfully built and nearly six feet tall, with broad shoulders, a heavy beard, and glinting steel-blue eyes, Longstreet had somehow gained a reputation as an excellent administrator and disciplinarian of his troops. But as it turned out, Longstreet performed best when he chose to obey the commands of a superior officer. An independent sojourn in North Carolina illustrated his inability to discipline and administer

Braxton Bragg: born North Carolina 1817; graduated U.S. Military Academy fifth in the 1837 class of fifty; appointed 2d lieutenant 3rd Artillery; promoted to 1st lieutenant in 1838 and to captain in 1846; participated in the Seminole War and won three brevet promotions for gallant conduct during the Mexican War; in 1849 mar-

ried Eliza Brooks Ellis, daughter of a Louisiana sugar cane planter; after routine garrison duty on the frontier, he resigned his brevet lieutenant colonelcy in 1856 to become a Louisiana sugar planter; in 1861 appointed Confederate brigadier general and assigned to Pensacola, Florida, where he changed the volunteers he found there into drilled and disciplined soldiers; promoted to major general and assigned command of the Gulf Coast from Pensacola to Mobile; in 1862 he received orders to move his troops by rail to join General A. S. Johnston's army at Corinth, Mississippi, for the Battle of Shiloh, during which Bragg served as army chief of staff and commanded a corps; after Johnston's death, upon the recommendation of his successor, General P.G.T. Beauregard, Bragg was promoted to full general; in June he in turn replaced General Beauregard when that officer took an unauthorized sick leave; deciding to invade Kentucky, Bragg moved the bulk of his army from Tupelo, Mississippi, to Chattanooga, Tennessee, by rail, and then joined

an army. Longstreet's troops behaved so badly that Governor Zebulon B. Vance, in reporting disaffection among the people in his mountain counties, complained to President Jefferson Davis that in addition to "tories and deserters burning, robbing, and murdering,…they have been robbed and eaten out by Longstreet's command, and have lost their crops by being in the field nearly all the time trying to drive back the enemy." Vance did not specify whom he meant by "the enemy"— Longstreet's marauding troops, the Federals, or both.

Longstreet's poor showing at the Battle of Gettysburg foreshadowed his performance of his duties, bordering on the insubordinate, while serving with the Army of Tennessee.

General E. Kirby Smith in a bold invasion of Kentucky; checked at Perryville in October by General D.C. Buell, Bragg retreated to Murfreesboro, Tennessee, where he fought a bloody battle against General W.S. Rosecrans in late 1862 and early 1863; Rosecrans's Tullahoma Campaign in June 1863 compelled Bragg to abandon Tennessee, but after receiving General James Longstreet's Corps from Virginia in September as reinforcements for the Battle of Chickamauga, he drove the Federals back into Chattanooga and began a siege that lasted until General U.S. Grant arrived from Mississippi in November 1863 and drove the Confederates back into Georgia; relieved of command of the Army of Tennessee, Bragg became President Davis's military adviser in February 1864; he exercised considerable power and served the president and the Confederacy well during the eight months he held this position, but his appointment came too late in the war for him to have a determinative impact; in January 1865, while still serving as the president's military adviser, Bragg engaged in his most ineffective performance as a field commander: he failed to prevent the Federals from taking Fort Fisher, which protected Wilmington, North Carolina, the last Confederate port open to blockade runners; Bragg spent the last weeks of the war under the command of General J.E. Johnston attempting to check General W.T. Sherman's advance; Bragg and his wife were part of the Confederate flight from Richmond until their capture in Georgia; Bragg, who lived in relative poverty after the war, died in Galveston, Texas, in 1876, and is buried in Mobile. Never a great field commander, he had talents the Confederacy needed but seldom used: the army possessed no better disciplinarian or drillmaster; an able organizer and administrator, he excelled as an inspector, possessed a good eye for strategy, and proved himself a dedicated patriot.

Longstreet tried to convince Lee to withdraw from Gettysburg before the battle began. He believed the Southern army should be positioned between the Federal army and Washington, D.C., on terrain more conducive to a Confederate victory. Lee, as usual, preferred the head-on approach. Having failed to persuade Lee to his own plan of battle at Gettysburg, Longstreet sulked. On July 2, 1863, after long delays and procrastination, his troops, moving forward along the Emmitsburg Road, found the situation different from what Lee supposed it to be when he issued orders for the advance. When informed of the new circumstances, Longstreet stubbornly insisted that Lee's original orders be carried out. A staff member later wrote that had Longstreet acted properly, instead of "pottering around in sullen inactivity," they could have seized Little Round Top, a key point of high ground, before the Federals did.

Robert E. Lee: born Virginia 1807; son of Ann Hill (Carter) Lee and Henry "Light-Horse Harry" Lee, who died when Robert was eleven; received early education in Alexandria, Virginia, schools; graduated second in his class at U.S. Military Academy in 1829, without receiving a demerit in four years; appointed 2d lieu-

tenant of engineers in 1829, 1st lieutenant in 1836, and captain in 1838; served at Fort Pulaski, Fort Monroe, Fort Hamilton, and superintended engineering project for St. Louis harbor; married Mary Ann Randolph Custis, whose father's estate of "Arlington" on the Virginia shore of the Potomac opposite Washington became Lee's home in 1857 after the death of his father-in-law; in 1846 Lee, then a captain, joined General Winfield Scott's Vera Cruz expedition and invasion of Mexico; Lee's extraordinary industry and capacity won him a brilliant reputation and the lasting confidence and esteem of Scott; wounded in 1847, Lee won three brevet promotions to major, lieutenant colonel, and colonel for gallant and meritorious conduct in the battles of Cerro Gordo, Contreras, Churubusco, and Chapultepec; served as superintendent of the

On July 3, Longstreet continued to pout. Under orders from Lee, he reluctantly took command of what became known as Pickett's Charge, but only half-heartedly carried out his responsibilities. In the ultimate act of removing his active support and denying responsibility, Longstreet took himself off for a nap, leaving it to his chief of artillery to order the advance when and if he thought it appropriate. When the attack failed, Lee shouldered the entire responsibility, allowing Longstreet to bask in his supposed innocence. But that was Lee's way with his subordinates. He seldom, if ever, confronted them with their shortcomings. It was easier to accommodate himself to their mistakes and faults, or to simply transfer them elsewhere.

Lee seldom allowed troops from his Army of Northern Virginia to be sent elsewhere, but he seemed to mount no

U.S. Military Academy from 1852 to 1855; promoted to lieutenant colonel 2d Cavalry in 1855; commanded Marines sent to Harper's Ferry to capture John Brown after his raid; promoted to colonel 1st Cavalry in 1861; having refused command of Federal armies, his first Confederate command led to failure at Cheat Mountain in western Virginia; after serving along the South Atlantic coast, he returned to Virginia as military advisor to President Jefferson Davis until June 1862 when he replaced the wounded Joseph E. Johnston in command of forces that became known as the Army of Northern Virginia; for nearly three years, Lee's aggressive campaigns and effective defenses frustrated Union efforts to capture the Confederate capital; not until February 1865—two months before his surrender—did he become over-all commander of Confederate forces; after the war, he accepted the presidency of Washington College (later changed to Washington and Lee University) in Lexington, Virginia, where he remained until his death in 1870. Theodore Roosevelt proclaimed Lee "without exception the very greatest of all the great captains." "Lee possessed every virtue of other great commanders without their vices," announced an orator. "He was a foe without hate; a friend without treachery; a victor without oppression, and a victim without murmuring. He was a public officer without vices; a private citizen without reproach; a Christian without hypocrisy and a man without guile." Bold, modest, and heroic, Lee once confessed that if war were less terrible he would become too fond of it. His greatest biographer characterized him as "a simple gentleman."

objections to the departure of Longstreet and his corps. Possibly he merely acquiesced to Longstreet's own desires, as Longstreet had campaigned long and hard for a transfer to the West. But there is evidence that his commander led Longstreet to believe that he might win the Army of Tennessee. Later, in response to a fawning letter from Longstreet suggesting that Lee himself should come west to command, Lee responded, "I think you can do better than I could. It was with that view I urged your going."

Then again, after Longstreet's performance at Gettysburg, Lee may have been relieved to be rid of the sulking subordinate.

2
CHICKAMAUGA

Longstreet's train chugged into Catoosa Station in the middle of the afternoon on September 19, 1863. Disgruntled that Bragg, deeply involved in a horrific fight, had not sent someone to greet him, Longstreet finally saddled his horse and set off toward the sounds of battle. Nine hours later, by the light of a brilliant moon, he arrived at army headquarters, a distance of ten miles from Catoosa Station.

At dawn Longstreet set out to find his command on the left of the Confederate line and began adjusting it to his satisfaction. Bragg had ordered a dawn attack to begin on the right under the command of General Polk and to then be taken up in a wave to the left. Bragg directed Longstreet to wait for Polk's action on the right and then to attack promptly so the entire Confederate line could roll the Federals into the inescapable trap of McLemore's Cove. The plan hinged on Polk following orders, something he had never done in the past, and did not

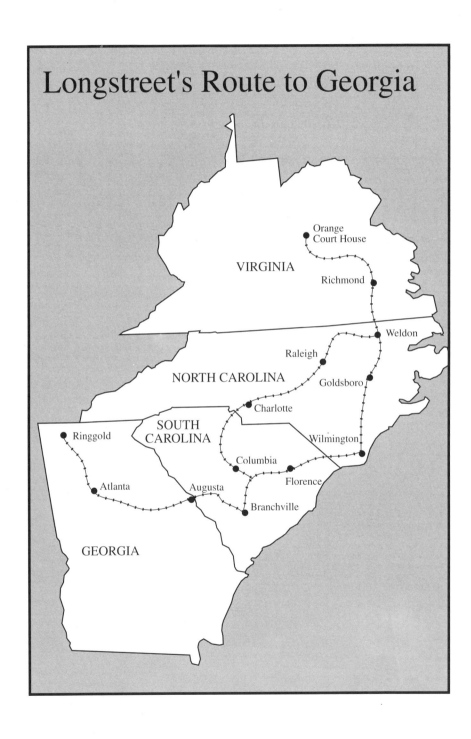

do now. Long after the attack should have been underway, Polk remained at his ease on the porch of his headquarters enjoying a leisurely breakfast and reading the newspaper. By the time things were sorted out and the Confederates began the attack, it was already mid-morning.

The Federals, too, suffered from confusion in their lines. On the Union right, facing Longstreet's position, a division of soldiers was inadvertently moved, creating a huge gap in the line precisely where Longstreet's columns were poised to attack.

When the moment for the assault came, Bragg's orders began the advance, but judicious troop deployment furthered its success. Longstreet had arranged the troops on a narrow front, achieving the effect of one large column striking the center of the Union line. General John Bell Hood, commanding Longstreet's lead column, smashed the Federal line near the Brotherton House and quickly wheeled to the right, giving the dismayed northerners a nasty surprise. Although Hood

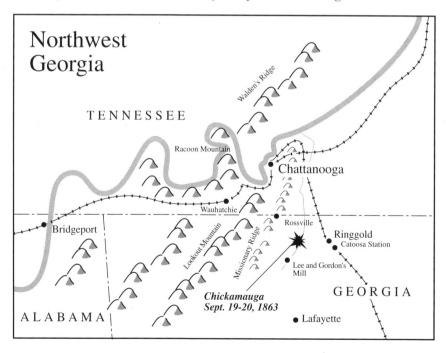

received a wound that put him out of the fight, and cost him his leg, his troops, along with others, pressed the enemy, who fled for their lives toward Chattanooga. The few Federals who did not flee soon found themselves isolated on the heights of Snodgrass Hill under the command of General George Thomas.

Leonidas Polk: born North Carolina 1806; attended the University of North Carolina and then the U.S. Military Academy, graduating eighth in his class of thirty-eight in 1827; brevetted 2d lieutenant and posted to artillery, Polk served only a few months before resigning to study for the Episcopal ministry; ordained a deacon in 1830, he became Missionary Bishop of the Southwest in 1838 and Bishop of Louisiana in 1841; assisted in the establishment of the University of the South at Sewanee, Tennessee; at the outbreak of the Civil War, Polk accepted a major general's commission from his close friend Confederate President Jefferson Davis;

Polk's departmental command consisted of parts of Arkansas and western Tennessee; he committed a disastrous error in violating Kentucky's neutrality by occupying Columbus in September 1861, opening that state to Federal invasion; commanded a corps with gallantry but little skill at Shiloh and in the invasion of Kentucky; promoted to lieutenant general in October 1862, he directed a corps at Murfreesboro and a wing at Chickamauga; his overt criticism of General Braxton Bragg resulted in his banishment from the Army of Tennessee; he was given command of the Department of Alabama, Mississippi, and East Louisiana where he remained until ordered, in May 1864, to join the Army of Tennessee, now headed by Bragg's replacement General J.E. Johnston; Polk led his army (in effect, a corps) during the opening stages of the Atlanta Campaign; on 14 June 1864 he was instantly killed when struck by a solid shot while surveying Federal positions from Pine Mountain near Marietta, Georgia. General Polk's impact on the Confederate cause was largely negative. His violation of Kentucky neutrality proved irreparable and his feud with Bragg severely damaged the effectiveness of the Army of Tennessee. Davis's reluctance to remove Polk only exacerbated the situation.

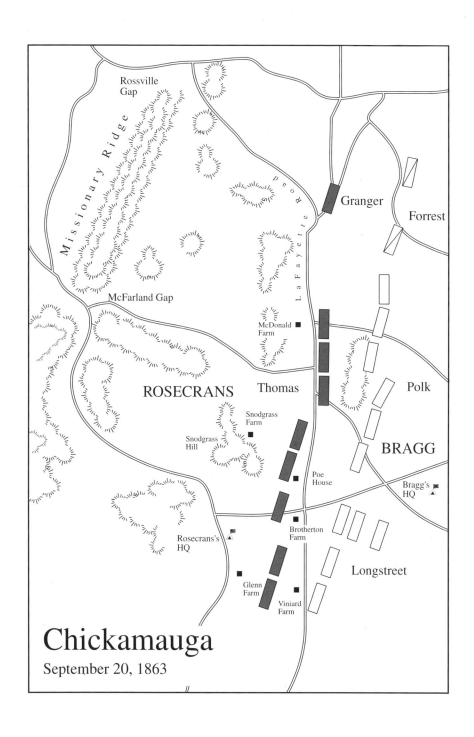

Rossville
Gap

Missionary Ridge

McFarland Gap

LaFayette Road

Granger

Forrest

McDonald
Farm

ROSECRANS

Thomas

Polk

Snodgrass
Farm

Snodgrass
Hill

BRAGG

Poe
House

Bragg's
HQ

Rosecrans's
HQ

Brotherton
Farm

Longstreet

Glenn
Farm

Viniard
Farm

Chickamauga
September 20, 1863

Thomas's heroic stand, which bought time for the remainder of the Union Army to reach the relative safety of Chattanooga, earned him the sobriquet "Rock of Chickamauga."

Longstreet realized that if he could seize Snodgrass Hill he would be "complete master of the field." He ordered the attacks continued until, with the enemy "crippled...so badly that his ranks were badly broken,...by a flank movement and another advance the heights were gained." In his report, Longstreet boasted: "The enemy had fought every man that he had, and every one had been in turn beaten."

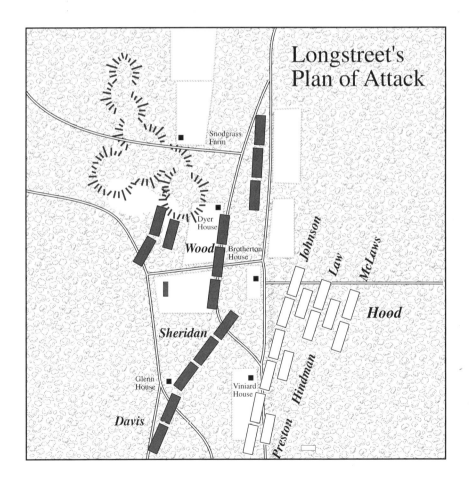

Longstreet's
Plan of Attack

Snodgrass
Farm

Dyer
House

Wood   Brotherton
House

Johnson

Law

McLaws

Hood

Sheridan

Hindman

Glenn
House

Viniard
House

Davis

Preston

General Arthur M. Manigault, commanding a mixed brigade of South Carolinians and Alabamians in the advance, confirmed Longstreet's statement regarding the ferocity of the fighting. "Again and again [we] were...driven back, but as promptly rallied and moved forward again," Manigault declared. "Nothing but the determined valor of our soldiers could have withstood the withering volleys poured into them by the enemy who...fought with great obstinacy."

One of Manigault's soldiers, Joshua K. Callaway of the 28th Alabama, in turn confirmed the impressions of both of his

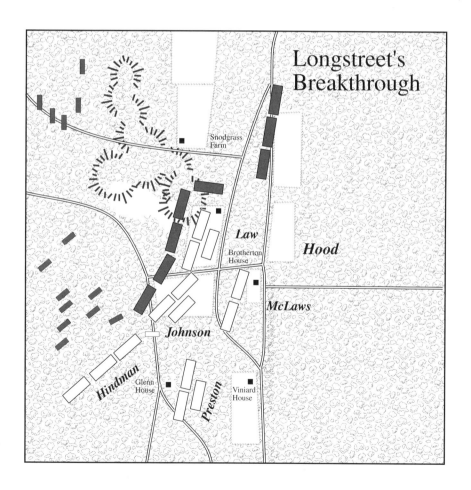

commanders in a lengthy eyewitness account of the fighting to his wife, Dulcinea:

> We threw out a line of skirmishers…and moved steadily forward not knowing how far off the enemy was. When we had gone about three hundred yards our skirmishers encountered those of the enemy, and as soon as the

Arthur M. Manigault: born South Carolina 1824 to a prominent family; a commission merchant and planter in and near Charleston, he was active in the state militia and served in the Mexican War; following the secession of South Carolina, he entered Confederate service; as a staff officer under General P.G.T. Beauregard he was present at the bombardment of Fort Sumter; selected colonel of the 10th

South Carolina Infantry; sent to the Western Theater, Manigault's regiment joined the Army of Tennessee in May 1862; after directing a brigade at Murfreesboro, he was promoted to brigadier general in April 1863; commanded a brigade in General James Longstreet's Wing at Chickamauga in September 1863; led his brigade at Chattanooga and throughout the Atlanta Campaign; during the Battle of Atlanta in July 1864 Manigault's Brigade spearheaded an assault that pierced the Federal line and threatened to divide the Union Army; during General J.B. Hood's ill-fated Tennessee Campaign, Manigault received a severe head wound at the Battle of Franklin in November 1864, ending his service to the Confederacy; after the war he returned to planting; in 1880 he became the adjutant and inspector general of South Carolina; General Manigault died in 1886 of the lasting effects of his Franklin wound. He was a capable commander and his brigade was among the finest in the Army of Tennessee. His memoir, *A Carolinian Goes to War*, not published until 1983, is an excellent account of activities in the Western Theater. The breakthrough of Manigault's Brigade during the Battle of Atlanta is the focus of that city's Cyclorama exhibit.

firing commenced all order and control was lost, the men raised the "war whoop," "the yell," "the battle cry" and away they went like a gang of mad tigers or demons...in double quick time. We soon ran over our skirmishers and those of the enemy fled as if old Scratch [the devil] had been after them. Thus we charged fully half a mile across [two fields]...and into another skirt of woods, with three [of] our Regiments on the right of the Brigade in a corn field perfectly exposed to the

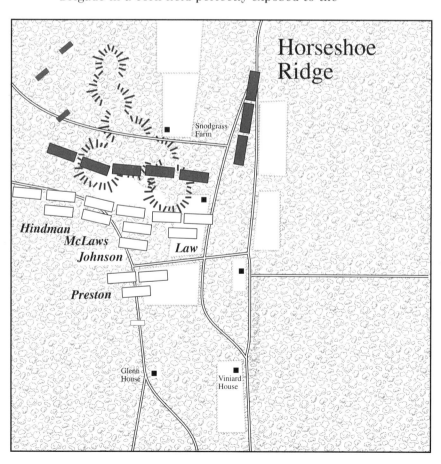

enemies' small arms and artillery which they could not stand long but gave way, and then all the enemies' fire was turned upon the 28th and 34th which we didn't stand long. But away we all went [in retreat] as fiercely as we had gone up there.

One piece of our artillery was left on the field and when Col. [John C.] Reid [commanding the 28th Alabama] asked for two companies to volunteer to go back and bring it out, Captain [Francis M.] Hopkin's Company and ours volunteered and we went back right in the face of the enemy and brought it off and as the Yankees saw fit to let us alone we did them and so it was done without the fire of a gun. Our Brigade [moved]...farther to the right and formed at the foot of a long hill on the top of which was the enemy's line. It was 2 o'clock in the evening and the battle was raging all along the line on our left and right as if heaven and earth were coming together. A thousand thunderstorms all turned loose together could not equal the noise.

We were now ordered forward and when we got half way up the hill [Snodgrass Hill] they opened on us with great fury with grape and canister and with small arms. But we moved steadily on till we got in about twenty yards of their line where we halted and went regularly to work. Here commenced a scene that beggars description, and God forbid that I should ever have to witness such another. The carnage was awful. Men were shot down all around me. I was indeed in the very midst of death. We fought them thus close I suppose about ten minutes when, as if by command, our whole line gave way and away we went down the hill like a gang of sheep. There was no line in our rear to support us. We fell back about two hundred yards and rallied and then advanced again to within about fifty yards of our former position when the Regt, on our left gave way again and the Yankees swung round into their place giving them a complete cross fire on the 28th. But we held the ground fifteen or twenty minutes and gave way again, but rallied as before and moved a third time to the charge. This time we reached the crest or top of the hill and found ourselves on equal footing with the enemy. Here we stood at least an hour before they gave way. (To give you some idea of how long we fought there I will relate a little incident: One man of our company, J. R. Smith, who stood in the very front of the fight, shot away all his 40 rounds and came back to me for more ammunition and I cut the cartridge box off of a wounded man and gave [it] to him and he went back & shot nearly or quite all that away; And that you may know he was not excited but brave & gallant I must tell you what he said while I was getting his ammunition: There were a good many lying back and skulking behind trees under the hill, and he bawled out to them "It's a free fight, boys, come up and pitch in." And just as I handed him the cartridge box a man came up the hill holl[er]ing at the top of his voice, to those who were lying back, to "Rally boys and fight for your country." and spoke to Smith as if he thought Smith was one of them [lying back],

and Smith took him by the arm and led him off
saying, "Come fight side of me, I'll see you
out." And led him off. But I soon lost sight of
him and don't know how long he stood up.)

The Yankees gave way about dark and fled
in every direction. We followed them over half
a mile, picking up a great many prisoners,
when another Brigade came up and followed
on after them.

We now..."Slept on the battle field"
Napoleon's sign of victory. But the Sleep of a
victorious army on a field won is not very
sweet when we are haunted all night long with
the groans and cries of the wounded dying.

I have now seen and experienced "The
horrors of war" as well as the spoils and glo-
ries. And may God deliver us from so awful a
scourge and calamity!

Having smashed the Federal line, the Confederates pursued
the enemy a short distance as they fled toward Chattanooga. A
Confederate captain recalled, "[W]hen we were ordered forward we raised a yell, and went at them at a double quick, but
they went [in retreat] at a double quicker. I tell you they
skedaddled in fine style."

Polk's failure to move as ordered in a timely manner thwart-
ed Bragg's plan to roll up the Federal Army. Nevertheless,
Bragg achieved the greatest victory the Confederates were
ever to accomplish in the Western Theater. But Longstreet saw
fit to disparage his commander's role in the battle. Although
Bragg remained on the battlefield directing and attempting to
coordinate the efforts of the two wings of his army, Longstreet
later charged that the commander had left the field. In his
1896 memoir, written long after Bragg's death, Longstreet
claimed that during the afternoon of the 20th, Bragg, upset by

the failure of his plan, refused to send reinforcements from Polk's command. "There is not a man in the right wing who has any fight in him," Longstreet quoted Bragg as saying just before he rode off the field to his headquarters at Reed's Bridge.

But Longstreet's report, made within a month of the battle, tells a different tale. No mention is made of Bragg leaving the field, and Bragg's headquarters were located at Thedford's Ford, not Reed's Bridge. In any case, Bragg's dispatches throughout the afternoon were headed "In the field." It appears that Bragg's alleged absence from the field is, in fact, a myth perpetuated by Longstreet and disseminated by others who have relied upon Longstreet's poor memory of events. Rather than leaving the field, Bragg remained with the right wing of the army. Longstreet himself reported that about the time his left wing broke up the enemy in their front, "the Right Wing made a gallant dash"—the one Bragg had repeatedly urged Polk to make—"and gained the line that had been held so long and obstinately against it." Moreover, in his memoir, Longstreet failed to mention his own reserves who had not yet been engaged in the fighting. Why he thought Bragg deserved condemnation for the failure to send reinforcements when he had fresh troops of his own that he did not throw into the battle is left unexplained.

3
CHATTANOOGA

The Federal army's complete withdrawal under cover of darkness from the bloody Chickamauga battlefield during the night of September 20–21 eventually led to further controversy among the Confederate high command. Bragg received much criticism for failing to recognize the extent of his victory. Longstreet's 1896 memoir is as suspect in this matter as it is on Bragg's whereabouts during the afternoon of the twentieth, and it directly contradicts his orders on the twentieth and twenty-first and his official report written in October 1863. Perhaps in his dotage Longstreet misremembered, but his sorry record of veracity on other occasions leads one to believe he deliberately distorted the facts.

In his memoir Longstreet sarcastically contended that Bragg "did not know of his victory until the morning of the twenty-first," twelve hours after the enemy's retreat, and suggested that he himself did know the Federals were gone. He

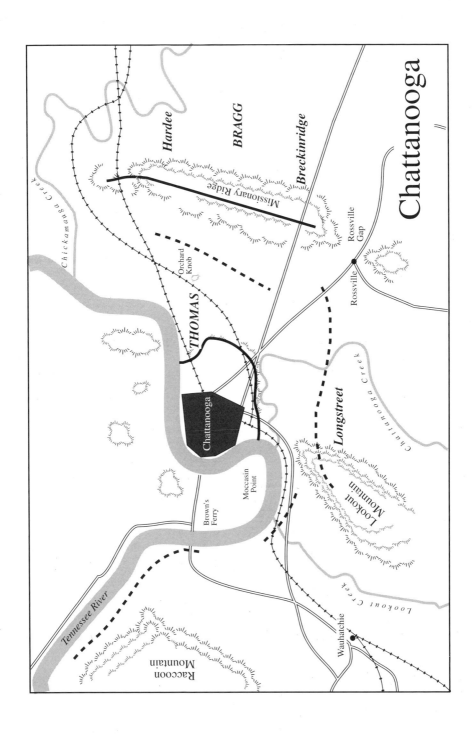

does not explain why, if he did possess this knowledge, he did not see fit to share it with his commander. His own dispatches to Bragg, however, give the lie to his later contention. At 6:15 P.M. on the twentieth Longstreet reported that he *believed* his command had been successful and he hoped to be prepared for a renewal of the fighting early the next morning. His early morning communications on the twenty-first even more explicitly reveal Longstreet's uncertainty as to the Federals' location. At 5:30 A.M. he ordered his cavalry to "ascertain the position of the enemy," and his 6:40 A.M. dispatch to Bragg reported, "I am much occupied in sending forward my lines of sharpshooters to find and feel the enemy." Longstreet, obviously, had no better knowledge of General William S. Rosecrans's complete withdrawal from the field than did Bragg. Other reports from the field commanders support the view that no one in the upper echelons of the Confederate army had any idea that they had completely driven the Federals from the field.

Besides the lack of information on the rout of the Federals, Bragg's army had become completely disorganized by the fierce battle. Confusion reigned among the ranks of the army at all levels, and supplies of all sorts needed replenishing. For the next three days, as order was reestablished, the Army of Tennessee cautiously closed on the Federals who were now firmly entrenched in Chattanooga. The Southern army took positions on the high ground—Lookout Mountain and Missionary Ridge—overlooking the city and the enemy.

When General Bragg set up his headquarters at the Noll House on Missionary Ridge he immediately began purging the army of those he believed, with good cause, to be incompetent. Polk had hindered every movement Bragg had attempted since becoming commander of the Army of Tennessee. The bishop-general displayed no inclination to follow anyone's orders, ever. He simply meandered his way through the war to the beat of his own drum until an enemy artillery shell removed him from this world on June 14, 1864, near Marietta, Georgia.

Hindman had failed Bragg at McLemore's Cove just prior to the Battle of Chickamauga by refusing to advance his troops despite explicit and repeated orders. Bragg also relieved General Daniel Harvey Hill, probably because of Hill's lack of support for his commander and a mutual dislike for one another. Bragg had earlier complained to Secretary of War Seddon that Hill's "open and constant croaking would demoralize any command in the world." Bragg's actions both exacerbated long-standing resentments and created new ones.

Within a short time, in retaliation, Bragg's high-ranking officers got up a petition to Davis that he be removed from command of the Army of Tennessee. The petitioners charged that Bragg had allowed the opportunity provided by the victory at Chickamauga to slip from his grasp, and that the Army of Tennessee would be fortunate to escape its present position without a disaster. They asked that Davis replace Bragg with someone who could inspire the army with confidence. Pretending they did not wish unduly to criticize Bragg, they suggested that his removal be based upon his poor health which, they contended, made him totally unfit for field command. The conspirators declared that their petition, although extraordinary, was prompted solely by their keen sense of responsibility, duty, and patriotism.

Although Generals Longstreet, Polk, D.H. Hill, Simon B. Buckner, Patrick Cleburne, and William Preston, among others, signed the petition, no one had the courage to claim authorship after the attempt to oust Bragg failed. Instead, through the years various participants tried to foist the responsibility on each other. Long after Polk was dead, Hill told Davis that Polk got it up and persuaded Buckner to write it, and the *Official Records* (the collected and published orders, reports, letters, etc., of the Civil War) acknowledge it is "supposed to have been written by Buckner." One historian contends that the evidence indicates that Longstreet acted as the chief inciter. General William Whann Mackall, a member of

Bragg's staff, informed his wife that Longstreet "is talking about him [Bragg] in a way to destroy all his usefulness," and a few days later he complained to General Joseph E. Johnston, "I think Longstreet has done more injury to the general than all the others put together." In addition, Lafayette McLaws, a subordinate of Longstreet, told Bragg in early 1864 that Longstreet helped form the coalition against him.

After Hill's death, Longstreet "revealed" that the petition "was written by General D.H. Hill (as he informed me since the war)," although Hill had emphatically denied having written it in an 1888 letter to Longstreet.

Whoever instigated the subterfuge, Bragg was their commander, and the petitioners owed him the outward forms of respect and professional loyalty. Further, it is unbecoming and unprofessional in a soldier to engage in conspiracy, and con-

Daniel Harvey Hill: born South Carolina 1821; graduated twenty-eighth of fifty-six at the U.S. Military Academy in 1842; appointed brevet 2d lieutenant 1st Artillery 1842; transferred to 3rd Artillery 1843; promoted to 2d lieutenant 4th Artillery

1845; 1st lieutenant 1847; served in Mexican War, brevetted captain for gallant conduct at Contreras and Churubusco, and brevetted major for meritorious conduct at Chapultepec; resigned from US Army 1849; professor of mathematics, Washington College, Virginia, 1848–54, Davidson College, North Carolina, 1854–59; he became superintendent of the North Carolina Military Institute at Charlotte from 1859 until the Civil War; elected colonel of the 1st North Carolina Infantry, which in June 1861 he led successfully at Big Bethel, Virginia; promoted to brigadier general, served in North Carolina, and returned to Virginia in 1862 as a major general; fought at Williamsburg, Seven Pines, and won praise from General R.E. Lee for his actions during the Seven Days; appointed commander of Department of North Carolina, but returned to division command in the Army of Northern Virginia

spiracy is precisely what these officers were about. Not only did they engage in conspiracy; none of them had the courage of their so-called convictions, as illustrated by their reluctance to admit to authorship of the petition.

When Davis heard of the petition he immediately sent an emissary, General James Chesnut, Jr., to investigate the situation. Chesnut no sooner arrived than Longstreet accosted him and urged that he convince Davis to replace Bragg. Chesnut quickly informed Davis of the situation and urged him to make a personal visit. Davis came.

Soon after his arrival, the president held a council of the dissatisfied generals with Bragg present. Longstreet's unreliable memoir would have us to believe that during the meeting he shied away from the subject of Bragg's removal. "After some talk, in the presence of General Bragg," Longstreet wrote, "[Davis]

shortly after Second Manassas; falsely accused of losing the Confederate battle plan in Maryland, he fought aggressively at Sharpsburg; poor health and failure to receive promotion to lieutenant general embittered Hill; he returned to administrative duties in North Carolina until in 1863 he accepted corps command in Braxton Bragg's Army of Tennessee; participated in combat at Chickamauga in September; engaged in bitter quarrel with Bragg in which President Davis favored Bragg and relieved Hill from command. Hill spent the rest of the war trying to clear his record, but could obtain only minor commands; in 1864 served as volunteer aide to General Beauregard; for a few days he commanded a division against Union General David Hunter at Lynchburg, Virginia; in 1865 Hill ended his military career by commanding the District of Georgia, fighting at Bentonville, North Carolina, and surrendering with General Johnston at Durham Station. After the war Hill published *The Land We Love,* a monthly magazine, 1866–69, and *The Southern Home*, during the 1870s; he also wrote a number of articles for Century Company's *Battles and Leaders of the Civil War;* in 1877 he became president of what would become the University of Arkansas; in 1885 he became president of Middle Georgia Military and Agricultural College; he resigned in 1889, dying of cancer in Charlotte on September 24. Contemporaries recognized Hill's "well deserved reputation as a hard fighter," but labelled him "harsh, abrupt, often insulting"—a man who would "offend many and conciliate none." He never resolved his quarrel with Davis and Bragg.

made known the object of the call, and asked the generals...their opinion of their commanding general, beginning with myself. It seemed rather a stretch of authority, even with a President, and I gave an evasive answer and made an effort to turn the channel of thought, but he would not be satisfied, and got back to his question." Longstreet then stated that he believed "our commander could be of greater service elsewhere than at the head of the Army of Tennessee." Another general reportedly told Davis that Bragg had lost completely "the confidence of the army, and...this fact alone destroyed his usefulness." As sharp and hurtful as

Simon Bolivar Buckner: born Kentucky 1823; graduated U.S. Military Academy 1844, eleventh in his class of twenty-five; brevetted 2d lieutenant of infantry, he

saw duty on the frontier and taught at West Point; promoted to 2d lieutenant in 1846, he joined General Winfield Scott's command in Mexico, where he was wounded at Churubusco and won brevet promotions to 1st lieutenant and captain; returned briefly to West Point as an instructor in infantry tactics; promoted to 1st lieutenant in 1851 and received the staff rank of captain in 1852; the bulk of his service was on the Western frontier until his resignation from the Army in 1855; Buckner engaged in real estate with his father-in-law in Chicago and managed his wife's substantial holdings; in 1858 settled in Louisville; active in the Kentucky militia, becoming inspector general in 1860; with the coming of the Civil War he worked to secure Kentucky's neutrality, declining a Federal brigadier general's commission proffered by President Abraham Lincoln and General Scott; although Buckner owned no slaves and opposed secession, he opted for the Confederacy following pro-Union posturing in the state legislature; appointed brigadier general in Confederate service in September 1861, he led a force that captured Bowling Green, Kentucky, shortly there-

these statements are, a staff officer declared, "Some others…did not handle the matter with the same delicacy of expression." Bragg must have been appalled and outraged. Longstreet does not explain why he would try to change the subject of the meeting. After all, that was why Davis was there, and that was the purpose of the meeting.

Longstreet later stated that on the following day Davis offered him command of the army, but that he turned it down. It is impossible to believe Longstreet would have turned down such an offer, and there is little doubt that Longstreet expect-

after; in February 1862, after senior officers J.B. Floyd and G.J. Pillow fled, Buckner surrendered Fort Donelson to his friend and West Point classmate U.S. Grant; imprisoned in Massachusetts until exchanged in August 1862; promoted to major general, he joined the Army of Tennessee; led a division in General Braxton Bragg's Kentucky invasion; given command of the District of the Gulf in December 1862 and the Department of East Tennessee in May 1863; rejoined Bragg's army and led a corps in General James Longstreet's Wing in the victory at Chickamauga; following that battle, Buckner joined a group of officers who called for Bragg's removal and may have penned the petition that many high-ranking generals signed; Bragg retaliated by reducing Buckner to division command and abolishing his Department of East Tennessee; a long illness kept Buckner from active duty until the spring of 1864; he served on the court martial of General Lafayette McLaws and declined the command of General J.B. Hood's former Army of Northern Virginia Division; transferred to the Trans-Mississippi and promoted to lieutenant general in September 1864, Buckner commanded the District of West Louisiana, served as chief of staff for General E. Kirby Smith, and surrendered along with Smith at New Orleans in May 1865; forbidden to leave Louisiana, Buckner worked as a commission merchant and newspaperman until allowed to return to Kentucky in 1868; able to recover his confiscated property in Kentucky and Chicago, he purchased the Louisville *Courier* and served as its editor for twenty years; governor of Kentucky from 1887 to 1892, vice presidential candidate on the "Gold Democrat" ticket in 1896, General Buckner died at his estate near Munfordville in 1914, the last surviving Confederate general above the grade of brigadier. Although he saw limited combat, Buckner performed credibly when given the opportunity. His involvement in the anti-Bragg faction no doubt damaged his career.

ed to replace Bragg as commander of the Army of Tennessee. Earlier, he had written Louis T. Wigfall, his mentor in the Confederate Congress, that General Lee would be reluctant to allow him to go to the Western army unless he were given a separate command. "But," Longstreet warned, "[Lee] will not

Patrick R. Cleburne: born Ireland 1828; served for three years in the British Army before purchasing his discharge and migrating to the United States in 1849; settling in Helena, Arkansas, he became a naturalized citizen; worked as a druggist and studied law, gaining admittance to the bar in 1856; in 1860 he helped organize a local militia company, the Yell Rifles, and became its captain; with the secession of Arkansas, Cleburne was elected colonel of a regiment that eventually became the 15th Arkansas; joined General William J. Hardee's command in the advance on Bowling Green, Kentucky, beginning a long association and friendship with that officer; promoted to brigadier general in March 1862, Cleburne led a brigade with

conspicuous skill at Shiloh; commanding a provisional division, he was instrumental in the Confederate victory at Richmond, Kentucky, where he was shot through the face; back with his brigade, he was again wounded at Perryville in October 1862; promoted to major general in December 1862, he led a division at Murfreesboro and Chickamauga; his command held its position on Missionary Ridge during the rout of General Braxton Bragg's Army of Tennessee and then covered Bragg's retreat; his stand at Ringgold Gap may have saved the army from destruction; his off-the-battlefield actions, however, cost him further promotion; he was an ardent member of the anti-Bragg faction calling for that general's removal and his proposal to arm slaves for service in the Confederate Army angered many, including President Jefferson Davis; Cleburne fought throughout the Atlanta Campaign, but was continually passed over for promotion; he was killed during the savage fighting at Franklin, Tennessee, in November 1864. General Cleburne was arguably the finest general officer in the Army of Tennessee and among the best to emerge during the war. He was one of only two foreign-born officers to become a major general in the Confederate Army.

be likely to consent to my going under any one else. Nor do I desire it." In addition, Longstreet had boasted that he could save the Confederacy if he were given command in the West. Now Lee seemed to encourage Longstreet. In response to Longstreet's disingenuous request that he come to Tennessee in the autumn of 1863, Lee reminded Longstreet of their mutual expectation of an independent command for Longstreet in the West. "The President, being on the ground," Lee wrote, "I hope will do all that can be done." But did Lee in fact conspire with Longstreet to help him gain command of the Western army? Again, one has to wonder if Lee seriously believed Longstreet capable of commanding the Army of Tennessee.

William Preston: born Kentucky 1816; he received a law degree from Harvard in 1838 and opened a practice in Louisville; during the Mexican War he served as lieutenant colonel of a Kentucky regiment; following the war, he served in both houses of the Kentucky legislature and in 1852 was elected to the U. S. House of Representatives, serving two terms; in 1858 he was appointed minister to Spain by President James Buchanan; upon his return to the U. S., he became a leading advocate of Kentucky secession; following the outbreak of the Civil War, Preston joined his brother-in-law General Albert Sidney Johnston at Bowling Green, Kentucky; appointed colonel and assigned to the staff of General John C. Breckinridge, he served in that capacity through the Battle of Shiloh in April 1862; promoted to brigadier general, he led a brigade at Corinth, Murfreesboro, and Chickamauga; in January 1864, whether owing to his diplomatic skill or his open criticism of General Braxton Bragg,  Preston was appointed minister to Mexico; unable to reach Emperor Maximilian, he spent the balance of the war in the Trans-Mississippi; following the war, he traveled to Mexico, England, and Canada before returning to Kentucky in 1866; he served two more terms in the state house and remained active in Democratic politics; General Preston died at Lexington in 1887.

There is no record of Lee ever suggesting such a move to Davis or any other Richmond decision-maker. It appears that Lee, in this instance, merely tried to soothe Longstreet's anxieties regarding his position.

But Longstreet had other powerful supporters. Senator

William W. Mackall: born Maryland 1817; graduated from the U. S. Military Academy in 1837, eighth in his class of fifty; brevetted 2d lieutenant and posted to artillery, he was severely wounded in the Seminole War; again wounded in the War with Mexico, he also won two brevets for gallantry; after the war his various duties included service on the Western frontier, in the Department of the East, and on the Pacific Coast; rising steadily through the ranks, he received in May 1861 the staff rank of lieutenant colonel together with an appointment as assistant adjutant general of the U.S. Army; however, he declined that position and resigned his Federal commission in July; shortly thereafter he entered Confederate service as a lieutenant colonel and became adjutant general to General Albert Sidney Johnston;

promoted to brigadier general in March 1862, Mackall was given the short-lived command of New Madrid and Island Number 10; surrendering the latter with 3,500 troops in April, he was imprisoned until exchanged in August 1862; held a succession of posts until he joined the Army of Tennessee as chief of staff to General Braxton Bragg in April 1863; although no fan of Bragg, he was not among the generals calling for Bragg's removal following the Battle of Chickamauga, but displeased with his own situation, Mackall resigned; he returned to the Army of Tennessee as chief of staff after General J. E. Johnston replaced Bragg in December 1863; when General J.B. Hood then replaced Johnston before Atlanta in July 1864, Mackall again resigned, discrediting himself by taking with him many of the headquarters records; he saw no further official duty, surrendering at Macon, Georgia, in April 1865; following the war he farmed in Virginia until his death in 1891. Although a capable staff officer, General Mackall was embittered by what he believed to be inadequate recognition by the Confederate government.

Lafayette McLaws: born Georgia 1821; graduated from the U.S. Military Academy, where he ranked forty-eighth among fifty-six graduates in the class of 1842; appointed brevet 2d lieutenant 6th Infantry 1842; 2d lieutenant 7th Infantry 1844; lst lieutenant 1847; captain 1851; served at various frontier posts; joined his uncle General Zachary Taylor to participate in the War with Mexico only to be transferred to General Winfield Scott's army at Vera Cruz, where McLaws became ill and returned home; in 1849 he married Emily Allison Taylor, a niece of General Taylor's; following the Mexican War, McLaws made the rounds of frontier posts until Georgia seceded in 1861; elected colonel of the 10th Georgia Infantry, McLaws took his new command to Virginia where he gained promotion to brigadier general; in 1862, he saw action at Yorktown before being promoted to major general in May; he fought at Antietam in September and defended Marye's Heights at Fredericksburg in December; his lack of initiative at Salem Church in May 1863 upset General Lee, and McLaws failed to receive either of the promotions to corps command in the Army of Northern Virginia following the death of Stonewall Jackson; at Gettysburg, McLaws became so incensed with Longstreet that he called him "a humbug, a man of small capacity, very obstinate, not at all chivalrous, exceedingly conceited, and totally selfish." Transferred along with

Longstreet to the West, McLaws found himself relieved of command during the Knoxville Campaign; when McLaws pressed for a court-martial, Longstreet charged him with improper preparations for an attack at Knoxville; the court's findings and its subsequent disapproval by President Davis produced "a vindication of McLaws and a humiliation of Longstreet." Sent to Georgia to defend Savannah, McLaws surrendered with Johnston's army after failing to halt Sherman's advance. Unable to make a living after the war, McLaws confessed: "I am without means, having lost all." He died July 22, 1897, in Savannah, Georgia. Douglas S. Freeman emphasized McLaws's "bad luck." He dragged along "on the road to Sharpsburg," noted Freeman; at Chancellorsville, he had "a chance to deliver a hammerstroke," but he hesitated; ultimately, McLaws had "no luster in the red glare of Gettysburg, though the fault is scarcely his."

Wigfall had been pressing Secretary of War James A. Seddon to replace Bragg with Longstreet, and he declared that fellow Senator James M. Mason shared his opinion. According to one of Longstreet's staff officers, Colonel John W. Fairfax, Seddon, too, supported the change in commanders. Fairfax reported that just before leaving for the Western army he had a visit from Seddon's brother. "When you get to the Army of Tenn[essee]," the visitor told him, "you will find Longstreet in command of the army." There can be little doubt Fairfax shared this prediction with his commander.

Upon his arrival at the Army of Tennessee, Longstreet had wasted no time in presenting himself for the position. After

Louis T. Wigfall: born South Carolina 1816; after attending a private military academy, he entered the University of Virginia in 1834, but left in 1835 to serve as a volunteer lieutenant in the Seminole War; graduated South Carolina College 1837; returned to University of Virginia to study law; admitted to the bar and practiced law in Edgefield, South Carolina, in 1839; an Episcopalian and a Democrat, he favored a society led by planters and based on black slavery and the chivalric code; appointed South Carolina militia colonel, he became known for his marksmanship, reckless courage, and thin-skinned sense of honor; gained a reputation for drinking, gambling, and economic carelessness; in 1840, as a result of some editorials he wrote, Wigfall became involved with the Preston Brooks family in a fistfight, three near-duels, two actual duels, and a shooting that left one man dead and two, including Wigfall, wounded; his neglected law practice dwindled, and despite his marriage to his respected second cousin, Charlotte Cross, he was nearly ruined socially, professionally, and financially; moved to Marshall, Texas, in 1848; elected to the Texas House of Representatives, he denounced Sam Houston, then a U.S. senator and strongly pro-Union, and advocated secession, just as he had in South Carolina; served in the Texas Senate from 1857 until elect-

only six days with the Western army he detailed Bragg's failings to Seddon. "This army has neither organization nor mobility, and I have doubts if its commander can give it them," Longstreet averred. "It seems he cannot adopt and adhere to any plan or course, whether of his own or of some one else." Of course, Longstreet contended that his sole concern was for the country: "In an ordinary war I could serve without complaint under any one whom the Government might place in authority," he would have Seddon believe, "but we have too much at stake in this to remain quiet.... I am convinced that nothing but the hand of God can save us or help us as long as we have our present commander." An apparently gullible clerk

ed to the U.S. Senate in 1859; as a fire-eater, Wigfall earned a reputation "for eloquence, witty but bitter debate, acerbic taunts, and a readiness for personal encounters"; he frequented "bars and gaming rooms, always seeking out adversaries"; he opposed the Federal Homestead Act because he believed that 160 acres was too small for a plantation with slaves, and "lampooned it as a bill that would provide land for the landless and homes for the homeless, but not 'niggers for the niggerless'"; warning that the South would never accept a Black Republican president, he boasted that if war came and "we do not get into Boston...before you get into Texas, you may shoot me." Wigfall, who helped thwart compromises to save the Union, resigned from the Senate in March 1861, refused an offer of the Texas governorship, becoming instead an aide to President Jefferson Davis, a Texas colonel, a Confederate colonel, and a member of the Confederate Provisional Congress; appointed a Confederate brigadier general late in 1861, but soon resigned to devote himself to his duties as Texas senator in the Permanent Confederate Congress, where he served from 1862 to 1865; favoring strong military measures such as conscription and impressment, he even voted to suspend the writ of habeas corpus, but Wigfall's confidence in President Davis continually decreased; the senator gave political support to Generals J.E. Johnston and P.G.T. Beauregard, and used his power to frustrate many of the president's plans; a more positive relationship between Wigfall and Davis might have allowed the executive and legislative branches to cooperate, but neither the president nor the senator was willing to compromise; after the war, Wigfall lived in London, where he tried to start a conflict between Britain and the United States, hoping this might revive an independent South; he returned to Texas and died at Galveston in 1874.

in Seddon's department, incredibly, believed Longstreet's letter "to be written without feeling and purely from a sense of duty."

Now, despite the determined efforts to dislodge Bragg, and the confrontation the president had insisted upon between Bragg and his subordinates, Davis upheld him as commanding general of the Army of Tennessee. In 1873 Davis explained to Bragg that his decision to retain him in command came about because "the conference satisfied me that no change for the better could be made in the commander of the army." The only realistic possibilities as replacements were generals Joseph E. Johnston or Gustave Toutant Beauregard, each of whom had by now lost Davis's confidence. General St. John Richardson Liddell, a Bragg subordinate, conceded, "Indifferent as Bragg

James A. Seddon: born Virginia 1815; graduated University of Virginia law school with honors in 1835; after being admitted to the bar in 1838, he practiced law in

Richmond; in 1845 married Sarah Bruce, daughter of a wealthy planter, and settled into the Clay Street mansion that later became the White House of the Confederacy; in 1845–47 and 1849–51, Seddon, an ardent follower of John C. Calhoun, served as a Democrat in the U.S. House of Representatives, where he supported state rights, the admission of Texas, the acquisition of Oregon, free trade, and the necessity of slavery to the southern way of life; fearing the loss of southern rights in the Union, he secretly favored secession and the formation of a southern republic; in the debate over the Compromise of 1850, he supported ultra-southern demands, siding with such extremists as Robert Barnwell Rhett, Sr., and Jefferson Davis; retired because of poor health to his Virginia plantation, but supported the ambitions of such friends as Robert M.T. Hunter; Seddon refused the nomination for vice president on the Buchanan ticket in 1856; he regarded the election of Abraham Lincoln in 1860 as the end of the South's territorial ambitions; counselling resistance to expected northern aggres-

was, I did not know of any better general to take his place."
When a nephew of Polk commented that "anyone would be better," Liddell challenged him "to name one, which he declined
doing."

Unable to oust him, several of Bragg's highest-ranking officers sought transfers, and some were reassigned. But
Longstreet remained, and Bragg's most serious and far-reach-
ing troubles would revolve around him. Longstreet had stopped
at nothing in his efforts to dislodge Bragg. His subversive
activities on his own behalf, and his refusal to carry out properly the responsibilities of a subordinate, boded ill for the
future of the Army of Tennessee, and for the Confederate
States of America.

sion, Seddon advised friends to prepare for the disruption of the Union; as a delegate to the Washington peace convention in 1861, he submitted a minority report
seeking a constitutional amendment protecting slavery in the Union, and throughout the debate vigorously defended southern interests; Seddon returned to
Richmond with ex-President John Tyler, also a delegate, to urge Virginia to secede
and join the Southern Confederacy; served in the Provisional Confederate
Congress, where he supported Jefferson Davis, before being appointed
Confederate secretary of war on November 21, 1862; from the war office Seddon
devised much of the South's offensive strategy of concentration, managed to
decentralize authority in the army, and created the Department of the West, but he
failed to work effectively with the Commissary Department or to successfully coordinate his ideas and policies with those of President Davis; resigned as secretary
of war on February 16, 1865, because of illness, and retired to his plantation;
imprisoned for a time after the war, he rebuilt his fortune through his law practice
and his plantations in Virginia and Louisiana; he destroyed his papers, fearing their
seizure by the Radical Republicans. In 1880 Seddon died on his Virginia plantation in Goochland County. He brought to the Confederate war office dedication
and intelligence as well as a tactful and an independent mind; a perceptive judge of
men, Seddon impressed diarist Mary B. Chesnut as warm and caring and a fasci-
nating conversationalist; without political ambition, diplomatic, and unselfish, he
was at his best as a sympathetic listener and a convincing advocate; he worked
hard, despite poor health and a cadaverous appearance; indeed, he was one of
Jefferson Davis's ablest advisers.

4
WAUHATCHIE

As the Confederate army established itself on the heights overlooking Chattanooga, Bragg positioned Longstreet at Lookout Mountain. All of the Federal lines of communication—the railroad, the river, and the wagon road—merged at the foot of Lookout Mountain, and Bragg depended upon Longstreet to disrupt the short "Cracker Line" of supply into the city. Bragg ordered the artillery to cut the line, and directed Longstreet to post sharpshooters along the river road on the north bank of the Tennessee in order to close that route to the enemy. He also granted Longstreet discretionary powers to take any other measures he thought necessary to achieve this goal. With success, the Federals would be forced to transport all of their necessities through a roundabout and difficult mountainous terrain.

Despite Longstreet's sarcastic remarks implying that the artillery and the sharpshooters merely got some "practice"

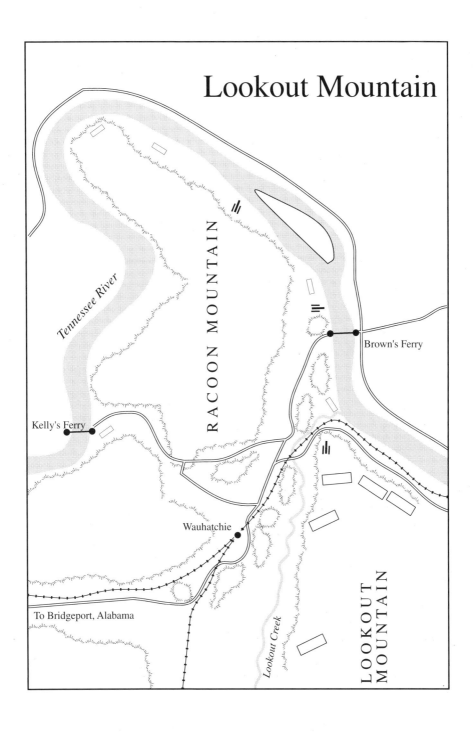

Lookout Mountain

Tennessee River

RACOON MOUNTAIN

Brown's Ferry

Kelly's Ferry

Wauhatchie

To Bridgeport, Alabama

Lookout Creek

LOOKOUT MOUNTAIN

from their activities, he did admit it put the Federals on shorter rations. Shorter rations were mighty slim indeed. "Bragg is now trying to cut off our supplies," a Federal complained to his wife in late September. "We are now hard up & hope we will not be compelled to do on less." A week later, however, he reported that both men and horses were on half rations.

Despite the importance of his responsibilities in the Lookout Mountain sector, Longstreet displayed a highly cavalier attitude toward his area of command. In later years he even denied that Bragg had entrusted him with responsibility for this important position. Longstreet nonchalantly ignored Bragg's directives and his own responsibilities while the Federals received reinforcements and a new commander. On October 19, on orders from Washington, D.C., Rosecrans turned his command over temporarily to General George

George H. Thomas: born Virginia 1816; graduated U.S. Military Academy 1840, twelfth in his class of forty-two; assigned to artillery, he served on the frontier and in coastal defenses; he fought in the Seminole War and earned two brevets in the

Mexican War; returning to West Point, he taught artillery and cavalry tactics; rising steadily through the ranks, Thomas became, in 1855, the junior major in the newly formed 2d Cavalry Regiment, an elite unit that included such future Civil War generals as A.S. Johnston, R.E. Lee, E. Kirby Smith, J.B. Hood, W.J. Hardee, Earl Van Dorn, and George Stoneman; serving on the Indian frontier and in Texas, Thomas made lieutenant colonel in April 1861 and was colonel when the 2d was redesignated the 5th Cavalry at the outbreak of the Civil War; although a Virginian, he remained loyal to the Union and was appointed brigadier general of U.S. Volunteers in August 1861; after serving briefly in the Shenandoah Valley, Thomas transferred to the Western Theater; he fought at Mill Springs, Kentucky, Shiloh, Corinth, and Perryville; promoted

Thomas, who held it only until the twenty-third, when General Ulysses S. Grant arrived to take permanent command. Three days later Grant set in motion plans laid by Rosecrans aimed at reopening the short supply line.

The Federal operation met with full cooperation from Longstreet. Learning of a probable Federal movement in the vicinity of Bridgeport on October 25, Bragg ordered Longstreet to make a reconnaissance, an order Longstreet disregarded. Early on the morning of the twenty-seventh Federal troops crossed the river and established a strong position near Brown's Ferry with no challenge whatsoever from Longstreet. Once again Bragg ordered Longstreet to investigate, report the strength and position of the enemy, and take whatever action was necessary to dislodge the Federals.

On the morning of the twenty-eighth Bragg rode to Lookout

to major general of volunteers in April 1862, he commanded a division at Stone's River; in September 1863 he commanded a corps during the Battle of Chickamauga, where he gathered the remnants of General W.S. Rosecrans's shattered force and held his ground long enough to prevent the army's total destruction; for this he earned the sobriquet "The Rock of Chickamauga"; promoted to brigadier general in the regular army in October 1863, he was given command of the Department and Army of the Cumberland; during the struggle for Chattanooga his command, acting without orders, drove the Confederates from Missionary Ridge; Thomas's Army of the Cumberland comprised more than half of General W. T. Sherman's force during the move on Atlanta in 1864, fighting steadfastly throughout that campaign; detached to oppose General J.B. Hood's strike into Tennessee, Thomas routed Hood at Nashville in December 1864; promoted to major general in the regular army shortly thereafter, he also received the thanks of Congress for Nashville; after the war he remained on duty in Tennessee before assuming command of the Department of the Pacific; General Thomas died at his headquarters in San Francisco in 1870. Although his slow, methodical approach often frustrated his superiors, Thomas was among the very best general officers to surface, on either side, during the war. Both Sherman and Grant downplayed Thomas's contribution to their success. That notwithstanding, his record reveals the important role he played in the Federal victory.

Mountain to observe the carrying out of his orders. Upon arrival, he discovered nothing to observe, and Longstreet nowhere to be seen. He sent a staff officer to find him. Longstreet was finally located at 9:00 A.M. at his camp, two or three miles from his line, enjoying his breakfast. General Liddell, joining Bragg in his vigil, reported that Longstreet eventually "came hastily up on foot," just as an artillery shell exploded close by. Unwilling to witness an exchange of hot words between his superiors, Liddell wandered off a short distance, where he soon spotted Federal soldiers moving through Raccoon Mountain to join those previously established on the

General Ulysses S. Grant: born Ohio 1822; graduated U.S. Military Academy 1843, twenty-first in his class; brevetted 2d lieutenant in 4th Infantry 1843; 2d lieutenant 1845; 1st lieutenant 1847; regimental quartermaster 1847 to 1853; brevetted captain 1847 for gallant conduct in Mexican War; assigned in 1852 to duty in

California, where he missed his wife and drank heavily; resigned from army in 1854 to avoid court martial; failed at a number of undertakings; appointed colonel 21st Illinois Infantry and then brigadier general volunteers in 1861; major general volunteers 1862; gained national attention following victories at Fort Donelson, Shiloh, and Vicksburg; received thanks of Congress and promotion to major general U.S. Army in 1863; after victories around Chattanooga, appointed lieutenant general and commander of all U.S. forces in 1864. Accompanied Meade's Army of the Potomac on a bloody campaign of attrition through the Wilderness, Spotsylvania, Cold Harbor, siege of Petersburg, and the pursuit to Appomattox; commander of the U.S. Army l864 to 1869; U.S. president 1869 to 1877. Visited Europe, suffered bankruptcy, and wrote his memoirs while dying of cancer; died in 1885 in New York City, where he is buried. "The art of war is simple enough," Grant once explained. "Find out where your enemy is. Get at him as soon as you can. Strike at him as hard as you can, and keep moving on." A staff officer said of Grant: "His face has three expressions: deep thought, extreme determination, and great simplicity and calmness."

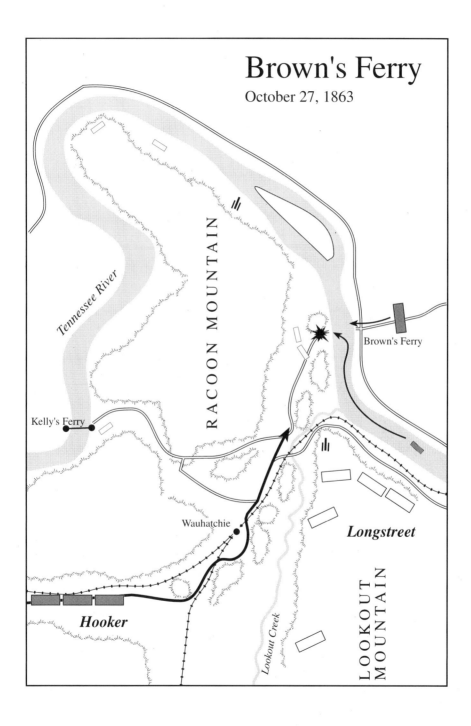

Brown's Ferry

October 27, 1863

south side of the river. When Bragg learned of these develop-
ments he became agitated, "very restless and complained with
bitterness of Longstreet's inactivity and lack of ability, assert-
ing him to be greatly overrated." Although Longstreet had been
amply forewarned of the enemy movements, he had made no

General Micah Jenkins: born South Carolina 1835; graduated in 1854 at the head
of his class from the Citadel; in 1855 cofounded King's Mountain Military School;
in 1856 married Caroline Jameson, whose father presided at the South Carolina
secession convention in 1860. Jenkins became colonel of the 5th South Carolina
Infantry in 1861; participated in the First Battle of Manassas; in 1862 he fought on
the Peninsula, at Seven Pines, and during the Seven Days' Battle, where he fre-

quently led General Richard H. Anderson's Brigade
and received praise for his gallantry from Generals
Joseph E. Johnston, James Longstreet, and Daniel
H. Hill; promoted to brigadier general in July,
Jenkins was severely wounded during the Second
Manassas Campaign at Chinn Ridge; he and his
brigade, part of General George E. Pickett's
Division, Longstreet's Corps, were at
Fredericksburg, but saw no combat; in 1863, after
accompanying Longstreet to Virginia south side
and participating in the Suffolk siege, Jenkins and
his men remained in Virginia and were not with
Pickett at Gettysburg. As senior officer, Jenkins
assumed command of Hood's Division, after Hood
was wounded at Chickamauga; following an unsuc-
cessful night attack at Wauhatchie, near Chattanooga, Jenkins and his principal
subordinate, General Evander M. Law, each blamed the other for the defeat; feud-
ing between Jenkins and Law continued during the Knoxville Campaign; in 1864
Jenkins, replaced as division commander by General Charles Field, returned with
his brigade to the Army of Northern Virginia; he was killed in the Wilderness on
May 6, 1864. General D. H. Hill said that at Seven Pines Jenkins's Brigade "ren-
dered more service than any two engaged." General Arnold Elzey considered
Jenkins "one of the most gallant & meritorious officers in the service." And
General Lee once told the brave and handsome Jenkins: "I hope yet to see you one
of my lieutenant generals."

plans, Bragg discovered, for an attack. The enemy forces simply moved up unchallenged to join those that had arrived earlier.

Chagrined at being caught out, Longstreet decided during the afternoon of the twenty-eighth to try to save face with a night attack on the Federal rearguard. Having been informed of the plans, Bragg reminded Longstreet that his entire corps was at his disposal to do with as he saw fit in the movement against the Federals, and, in addition, a division of Breckinridge's Corps was also subject to Longstreet's orders if they were needed. Longstreet later denied that he had had access to these troops, and, in fact, he employed fewer than 4,000 soldiers from just one division, that of General Micah Jenkins, to attack the 12,000 Federals.

Two separate battles took place on this bright, moonlit night. Jenkins's men, under the command of Colonel John Bratton, attacked the Federal camp commanded by General John W. Geary shortly after midnight. The Federals had been alerted to the impending assault, and as the Confederates neared the enemy they observed considerable commotion within the camp. "The hurrying hither and thither could be seen by the light of their campfires, which they were then extinguishing," Bratton testified.

Beginning on the Federal left, the fighting soon extended to three sides of the encampment. Geary reported that the Confederate commander "precipitately hurled his main body, without skirmishers, upon my left" where they met an intense fire. The Southerners "pressed forward vigorously...charge after charge was made...but each time the enemy's lines were hurled back under unintermitting fire" from both infantry and artillery, "that like a wall of flame opposed them." By 3:30 A.M. the Confederates withdrew. Geary noted with some relief, "Our victory was complete—the disasters to the enemy palpably extensive."

Meanwhile, General Evander McIvor Law's troops held a position atop hills overlooking the road along which Federal reinforcements might approach. Sure enough, General Oliver Otis Howard's Corps soon came marching down the thorough-fare. Although the Confederates surprised them with a flank attack, the Federals rallied and counterattacked. Holding their fire until they reached the Confederate line, they "made a gal-lant charge and took the crest." The Southerners, "without waiting to reply, retreated precipitately over the hill," abandon-ing their killed and wounded.

Longstreet's Battle of Wauhatchie, which resulted in nearly one thousand casualties, was ill conceived, ill planned, and poorly coordinated. In the end, it resulted in a shambles and a round of criminations and recriminations.

In his report, written six months after the event, Longstreet blamed Law for withdrawing his troops. Law, on the other hand, explained that he gave the order based upon his under-

Evander McIvor Law: born South Carolina 1836; graduated from the Citadel in 1856; taught, along with Micah Jenkins, with whom he later feuded, at Kings Mountain Military Academy in South Carolina from 1858 to 1860; moved to

Alabama, taught at a Military High School in Tuskegee, and studied law; in 1861 entered Confederate service as captain of a company, com-posed mainly of his students, that became part of the 4th Alabama Infantry; promoted to lieutenant colonel; seriously wounded at First Manassas, where his regiment's colonel died; promoted to colonel of the 4th Alabama; in 1862 he command-ed a brigade at Seven Pines and during the Seven Days' battles; praised on several occasions for leading his brigade at Second Manassas, Sharpsburg, and Fredericksburg; promoted in October to brigadier general; in 1863 Law married Jane Elizabeth Latta; at Gettysburg he initiated the attack on the Round Tops, and commanded General John Bell Hood's Division following the wounding of that general; Law also led Hood's Division in September at Chickamauga, where

standing of Longstreet's plan of operations. Longstreet, in turn, accused Law's troops of abandoning their position because of bitter jealousy among Jenkins's brigadier generals. However it happened, a soldier succinctly explained to his wife, "I have need to record another misfortune to our armies. Longstreet's forces allowed themselves to be surprised and we lost a great advantage we had over the enemy."

Longstreet also tried to place blame on the cavalry forces assigned to cooperate with him, claiming soon after the battle that Colonel Warren Grigsby failed to report to him as ordered. On November 3, Grigsby denied Longstreet's allegations, stating that Longstreet had issued no instructions for a reconnaissance, and that he had, indeed, reported the enemy's movements from Bridgeport and Shellmound to the general.

On the morning following the battle, Longstreet penned an

Hood was again wounded; afterwards, when temporary command of the division went to Jenkins, who ranked Law by three months, their rivalry became so intense that Law requested transfer to the cavalry and General Longstreet, who favored Jenkins, threatened to resign if Law was not court-martialed, but the War Department ignored the wishes of both men; in 1864 Law fought at the Wilderness, Spotsylvania, the North Anna River, and Cold Harbor, where he was severely wounded and his brigade repulsed an assault, inflicting more than 3,000 casualties on the Union Seventeenth Corps; after recovering from his wound, Law transferred to the cavalry; in 1865 he was promoted to major general and commanded General Matthew C. Butler's Division in the fighting at Bentonville, North Carolina; after the war, Law managed his father-in-law's estate, organized the Alabama Grange, and became associated with Kings Mountain Military Academy until it closed in 1881; he directed the South Florida Military and Education Institute from 1894 to 1903; edited the Bartow [Florida] *Courier-Informant* from 1905 to 1915, and served as a member of the Polk County Board of Education from 1912 until his death; he also played an active role in the affairs of Confederate veterans, serving as division commander of Florida from 1899 to 1903, helped organize a chapter of the United Daughters of the Confederacy in Bartow, and wrote several articles on the war. Law, the last of the Confederate major generals, died in 1920.

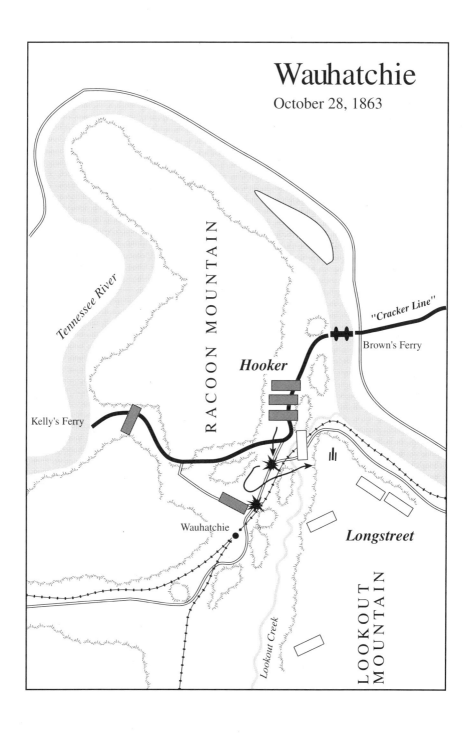

Wauhatchie
October 28, 1863

Tennessee River

RACOON MOUNTAIN

"Cracker Line"

Brown's Ferry

Hooker

Kelly's Ferry

Wauhatchie

Longstreet

Lookout Creek

LOOKOUT MOUNTAIN

amazing letter to Bragg's headquarters. He denied that he had intended to dislodge the Federals; rather he had merely desired to seize and hold a hill that commanded the enemy's road. To what purpose he did not state, as the position would have been too weak to be held for long by his forces. However, he went on confusingly, if the circumstances were favorable, he had planned to attack with his entire division and push the enemy into the river. When it became too late, in his opinion,

G. Moxley Sorrel: born Georgia 1838; brother-in-law of Confederate General W.W. Mackall, he worked as clerk for the Georgia Central Railroad and was active in Savannah's militia unit, the Georgia Hussars, with which he saw action during the capture of Fort Pulaski following Georgia's secession; anxious to enter Confederate

service, he traveled to Richmond, Virginia, where he received an appointment as captain and volunteer aide-de-camp to General James Longstreet; promoted to major in May 1862 and lieutenant colonel in June 1863; serving continuously with Longstreet from First Manassas to the Battle of the Wilderness, he held numerous posts including adjutant general and chief of staff of the First Corps; during the Battle of the Wilderness, Sorrel led three brigades (in effect, a division) in a highly successful flanking movement that turned the Federal left; in October 1864, with strong endorsements from Generals Longstreet, R.H. Anderson, and Robert E. Lee, Sorrel was promoted to brigadier general and given a brigade in General William Mahone's Third Corps Division; wounded at Petersburg and then severely wounded at Hatcher's Run, Sorrel was unable to rejoin the army before Lee's surrender in April 1865; after the war he returned to Savannah where he managed a steamship company and was a successful import/export merchant; General Sorrel died at Roanoke, Virginia, in 1901. His excellent memoir *Recollections of a Confederate Staff Officer* was published posthumously. Although frequently moody and overbearing, Sorrel was a superb staff officer and showed considerable ability when commanding troops in the field.

to begin a forward movement, he had left the field believing there was nothing to be done. Soon thereafter, he asserted, word came from General Micah Jenkins that a brigade was heavily engaged with Union troops. "I presume," Longstreet concluded hours after the engagement, "that little or nothing was accomplished."

In his first communication to Davis on the Wauhatchie affair, Bragg reported that it "strongly insinuates disobedience of orders & slowness of movements." In another message to Davis, Bragg described Longstreet's performance as "a gross neglect resulting in a most serious disaster." Davis expressed dismay at the report. "Such disastrous failure as you describe cannot consistently be overlooked," he wrote. "I suppose you

Edward Porter Alexander: born Georgia 1835; graduated U.S. Military Academy 1857, third in his class of thirty-eight; brevetted 2d lieutenant of engineers, he taught at West Point and then took part in the Utah Expedition; promoted to 2d lieutenant in 1858; with the secession of Georgia, he resigned his commission to

enter Confederate service as a captain; given direction of the signal corps, he served under General P. G.T. Beauregard at First Manassas; for a time he was Beauregard's chief of ordnance and later held that post under General J.E. Johnston; promoted to major in April 1862, his numerous duties in what became the Army of Northern Virginia included engineering, reconnaissance, and signal services; participated in the Peninsular Campaign and the Seven Days' Battles in the spring of 1862; elevated to lieutenant colonel in July, he frequently performed the tasks of incompetent Chief of Artillery General William Nelson Pendleton; Alexander ran the ordnance department during Second Manassas and Sharpsburg; a long-time advocate of organizing artillery into battalions, he received command of one of two battalions in General James Longstreet's Corps; Alexander's gun placements greatly contributed to the devasta-

have received the explanation due to the Government, and I shall be pleased if one satisfactory has been given." It was not.

The closest Longstreet came to taking responsibility for his failure appeared in the fairy-tale version of the war he produced in his memoirs. "It was an oversight of mine," he humbly confessed, "not to give definite orders for the troops to return to their camps before leaving them." Others have not been so gentle. "If anyone should bear the blame it is General Longstreet," concluded a recent article on the affair. Historian Thomas Connelly described the battle as a blundering disaster. The authors of one biography decided that Longstreet "was careless and handled matters poorly," while perhaps the kindest words came from another biography that confessed, with

tion of the Federal Army of the Potomac at Fredericksburg in December 1862; promoted to colonel the following spring, he assisted in the reorganization of the Army of Northern Virginia's artillery that paid dividends at Chancellorsville; at Gettysburg in July 1862, he directed the massive but largely ineffectual artillery barrage that preceded the Pickett-Pettigrew-Trimble charge; accompanied Longstreet's Corps to the Western Theater in September 1863, but arrived too late to see action at Chickamauga, Alexander participated in the battles around Chattanooga and at Knoxville before returning with Longstreet's Corps to the Army of Northern Virginia; promoted to brigadier general in February 1864, he became Longstreet's chief of artillery—a role he had performed informally for some time; fought throughout the Overland Campaign in Virginia and played a major role at Cold Harbor; assisted in the construction of the Richmond defenses and was wounded in the Siege of Petersburg; returning to duty, he fought at Drewry's and Chaffin's bluffs and served as de facto chief of artillery for the entire army; surrendered with General Robert E. Lee at Appomattox in April 1865; after the war Alexander taught engineering at the University of South Carolina, had a successful career in the railroad industry, engaged in planting, and held several public offices; he died at Savannah in 1910. General Alexander published *Military Memoirs of a Confederate* in 1907; a more detailed version written earlier for his family appeared in 1989 as *Fighting for the Confederacy*, these works remain among the finest and most useful Civil War participant accounts. Highly valued by Generals Lee and Longstreet, and President Jefferson Davis, Alexander was among the most gifted young Confederate officers.

fine understatement, that "the Longstreet of this period is not one to whom great deeds can be credited." General E.P. Alexander, Longstreet's chief of artillery, declared his commander guilty of "contributory negligence." The most generous and ingenious treatment of all came from Longstreet's chief of staff, G. Moxley Sorrel, who, in his recollections, virtually ignored all military activities during the entire month spent in Chattanooga, neatly jumping in his narrative from the battle of Chickamauga to Longstreet's later disasters.

5
KNOXVILLE

Longstreet's failure to hold his assigned position on the left
of the Confederate lines resulted in his separation from the
Army of Tennessee. On October 29 Davis suggested to Bragg
that Longstreet be assigned the task of pushing General
Ambrose E. Burnside out of East Tennessee. After the war,
Grant wondered why Longstreet's troops were sent away during this critical period at Chattanooga. "Knoxville was of no
earthly use to him while Chattanooga was in our hands," he
explained. Pointing out that if Chattanooga had fallen to the
Confederates Knoxville would have followed, he wrote, "I have
never been able to see the wisdom of this move." Grant failed
to understand the workings of the mind of Jefferson Davis,
who obviously believed the real Federal thrust would be
through East Tennessee into Virginia. Grant read Davis well
enough, though, to conclude that Longstreet was sent to
Knoxville "because Mr. Davis had an exalted opinion of his own

Ambrose Everett Burnside: born Indiana 1824; apprenticed to a tailor and worked in a shop until friends of his father, an Indiana legislator, secured him an appointment to the U.S. Military Academy, where he graduated eighteenth in the class of 1847; appointed 2d lieutenant in 3rd Artillery in 1847, but saw little service in Mexico; promoted to 1st lieutenant in 1851; married Mary Richmond Bishop of Rhode Island in 1852 and resigned from army a year later to manufacture a

breech-loading rifle he invented; company went bankrupt in 1857; major general in the Rhode Island militia and treasurer of the Illinois Central Railroad before the Civil War; in 1861 organized and became colonel of 1st Rhode Island Infantry, which was among the earliest regiments to reach Washington; became friend of President Lincoln and received promotion to brigadier general of volunteers in August 1861 after commanding a brigade at the Battle of Bull Run; in 1862 commanded a successful operation along the North Carolina Coast; commissioned a major general of volunteers and received awards and thanks from various states; at Sharpsburg he wasted too much time crossing Antietam Creek and attacking the Confederate right; after twice declining command of the Army of the Potomac, he finally accepted, although he considered himself incompetent and proved himself correct by crossing the Rappahannock River in December 1862 and making a disastrous attack on the awaiting Confederate army at Fredericksburg; "I ought to retire to private life," Burnside informed President Lincoln, who after relieving him of command in the East assigned him to command the Department of the Ohio; at Lincoln's urging, he advanced into East Tennessee and in November 1863 repulsed an assault on Knoxville by Confederates under James Longstreet; Burnside and his Ninth Corps returned to the East in 1864 to serve under Grant from the Wilderness to Petersburg; blamed by General George Meade for the Union failure at the Crater, Burnside shortly thereafter went on leave and never returned to duty; in 1865 he resigned his commission; after the war he became president of various railroad and other companies; elected governor of Rhode Island in 1866 and reelected in 1867 and 1868; elected to U.S. Senate from Rhode Island in 1874, where he served until his death at Bristol, Rhode Island, in 1881.

military genius....On several occasions during the war he came to the relief of the Union army by means of his *superior military genius.*"

Bragg later claimed he would have preferred to send someone else on the Knoxville expedition, but due to Longstreet's disobedience to orders he yielded to Davis's choice and sent his sulky subordinate instead. This statement, made ten years after the incident, does not jibe with what Bragg said at the time. On October 31, Bragg told Davis that the departure of Longstreet would be a great relief to him. He remarked to General Liddell that he had sent Longstreet "to get rid of him and see what he could do on his own resources." Moreover, Bragg was well aware of the folly of depending on Longstreet to carry out assignments in a reasonable and responsible manner, and probably did not injure his chances of holding the high ground around Chattanooga any more by sending him than by keeping him.

The campaign against Knoxville got off to a discouraging start. From the moment that he first received orders for the operation, Longstreet began complaining about the size of his force, the lack of transportation, and the vagueness of Bragg's instructions. He continually fussed and fumed about everything and everybody until Colonel George Brent of Bragg's staff concluded that it "looks as if he were preparing for a failure, & seeking in advance grounds for an excuse." Indeed, a letter Longstreet sent to General Buckner early in the expedition clearly indicated that he expected to fail. Longstreet obviously wished to escape blame even before anything occurred for which to blame anyone. Perhaps he foresaw the debacle of his independent command.

While General Joseph Wheeler's cavalry pushed ahead to probe the Knoxville defenses, Longstreet's soldiers plodded along the East Tennessee and Georgia Railroad. Nearly two weeks after leaving Chattanooga, the Southerners made their first contact with the enemy at Loudon, Tennessee. Here

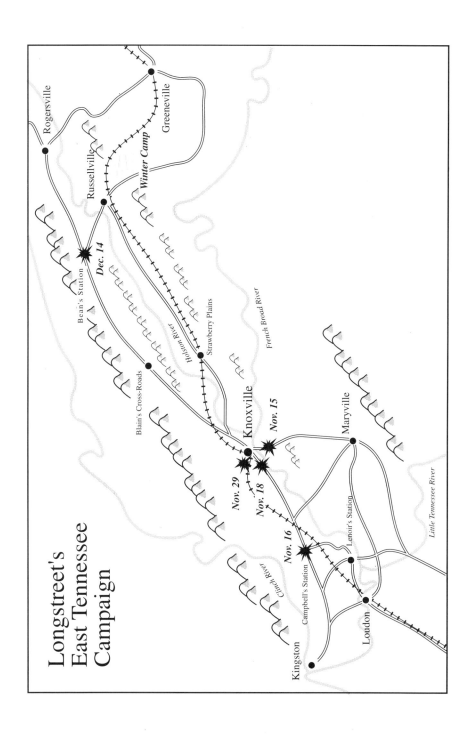

Longstreet's
East Tennessee
Campaign

Rogersville

Greeneville

Winter Camp

Russellville

Dec. 14

Bean's Station

Holston River

Strawberry Plains

French Broad River

Blain's Cross-Roads

Knoxville

Nov. 15

Maryville

Nov. 29

Nov. 18

Little Tennessee River

Lenoir's Station

Nov. 16

Clinch River

Campbell's Station

Loudon

Kingston

Burnside had Federal troops positioned to disrupt the railroad between Richmond and the West. Longstreet hoped to bring on a battle here on November 14, but Burnside quickly pulled his forces back.

Both armies now raced for Campbell's Station, a strategic intersection on the road to Knoxville. Winning the race by minutes on November 16, the Federals took up a strong defensive position. Longstreet's troops, however, had the opportunity to overlap the position, flanking both ends of the Union line. Unfortunately, General Evander Law's brigade, posted on the far right of the Confederate forces, failed to keep a proper alignment in its march, and ended up short of the Union left flank. The Federals spotted Law's brigade, recognized the threat to their position, and began pulling back. That night, under the cover of darkness, Burnside withdrew his troops. The next day they reached the safety of the Knoxville fortifications.

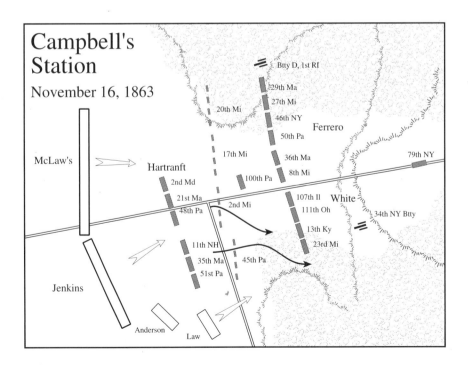

Campbell's Station

November 16, 1863

McLaw's

Jenkins

Anderson

Law

Hartranft

2nd Md
21st Ma
48th Pa

11th NH
35th Ma
51st Pa

20th Mi

17th Mi

100th Pa

2nd Mi

45th Pa

Btty D, 1st RI

29th Ma
27th Mi
46th NY
50th Pa

36th Ma
8th Mi

107th Il
111th Oh
13th Ky
23rd Mi

Ferrero

79th NY

White

34th NY Btty

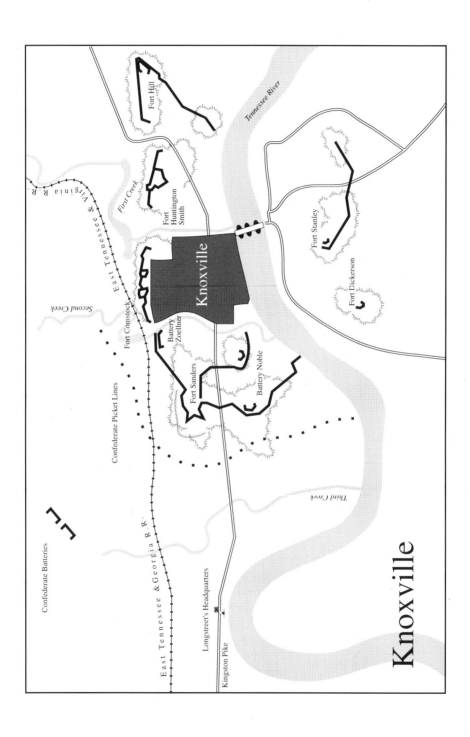

Knoxville

The affair at Campbell's Station had been Longstreet's best and last chance to destroy Burnside's army before it reached Knoxville, but through bungling, the opportunity slipped away. One of Longstreet's artillery officers later asserted, "If our infantry had been handled with anything like the skill and dash with which the artillery was handled...the greater part of Burnside's force would have been captured before he got to Knoxville." Law's division commander, General Micah Jenkins, with whom Law was not on friendly terms, reported that Law's mistaken march to position was a "careless and inexcusable movement" that "lost us the few moments in which success from this point could be attained." Longstreet, too, found Law a convenient scapegoat, and gleefully quoted in his memoir a staff officer's memorandum: "I know at the time it was current-ly reported that General Law said he might have made the attack successfully, but that Jenkins would have reaped the

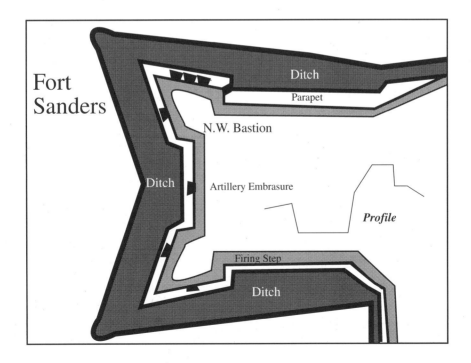

Fort Sanders
Ditch
Parapet
N.W. Bastion
Ditch
Artillery Embrasure
Profile
Firing Step
Ditch

credit for it, and hence he delayed until the enemy got out of the way." Longstreet no doubt found this a reasonable explanation for what had happened; after all, he himself had mismanaged responsibilities and assignments through pique and hubris.

On November 18, Longstreet, following closely on the heels of the Federals, began seeking the most favorable point upon

Fort Sanders

which to launch an assault. Some 1,400 yards in front of their main line, the Federal cavalry had built a long breastwork of fence rails, piled over three feet high and nearly as thick, behind which they had dismounted and taken a defensive position. Longstreet directed his chief of artillery, General Alexander, to dislodge them with his guns. The terrain made it possible for a number of Confederate gunners and two regi-

ments of South Carolina infantry to move undetected within several hundred yards of the Federals. The gunners opened fire, reported Alexander, "& immediately we could see rails flying in the air, & we afterwards found men killed behind them.... And, just as I had hoped, we could see the men deserting the breast work & running back...all along their line.... Within three minutes I gave the signal, & the infantry rose & charged with a yell....Our men advanced handsomely until they were within 40 yards of the breast work, when, to my surprise & disgust, they halted, laid down in the line of battle & began firing."

At that point an Irish gunner exclaimed, "Faith! & there goes the captain!" Captain Stephen Winthrop, an English adventurer serving on Alexander's staff, "immediately stuck in his spurs & was already nearly halfway to the infantry. I can see him now," recalled Alexander, "in a short, black, velveteen, shooting coat & corduroy trousers, with his rather short stout legs & high English seat in his saddle—his elbows square out, his sabre drawn—urging his horse almost into a run. But the officers of the infantry had already raised their men up....Then Winthrop dashed through a little gap in our line & right up at the breast work. As he did so we could see several carbines...spit smoke obliquely up at him & he suddenly fell forward on his horse's neck, & the horse turned about...& came back with him. He had gotten a bullet through the base of his neck tearing up the collar bone."

After driving the Federals back into their main fortifications, Longstreet considered various plans to oust them, but no sooner did he develop a stratagem than he changed his mind. He delayed mounting an attack for more than a week, while the Federals strengthened their defenses. Finally, on the night of November 28, Longstreet ordered troops into forward positions for a morning attack on Fort Sanders. Longstreet believed his possession of this fort, perched upon a hill, would be the key to overcoming the entire position. He informed

General Micah Jenkins, "I have no apprehension of the result of the attack if we go at it.... Keep your men well at their work, and do not listen to the idea of failing and we shall not fail. If we go in with the idea that we shall fail, we shall be sure to do so. But no men who are determined to succeed can fail."

The Confederates were indeed determined. "Moving slowly, but with zeal, and hope, and enthusiasm," their commander General Lafayette McLaws reported, "through a tangled abatis for about 15 yards, we came to comparatively open ground, where a rushing charge was made upon the fort." It was not an easy task. In addition to the abatis (outward-facing sharpened stakes) and a network of wires stretched along the ground, the attacking forces found a ditch around the fort. McLaws earlier had been assured by Longstreet and an engineer that the ditch would not present any difficulties. It was with some chagrin, then, that the troops found they could not overcome this barrier. During the cold night the wet sides of the ditch had frozen

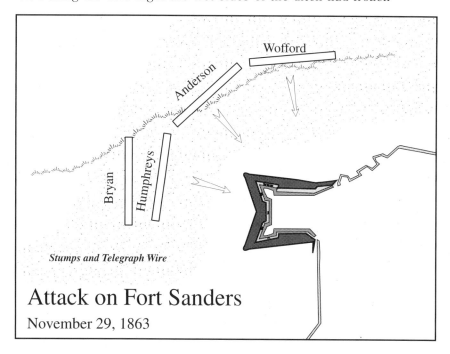

Wofford

Anderson

Bryan

Humphreys

Stumps and Telegraph Wire

Attack on Fort Sanders
November 29, 1863

into a sheet of ice.

As the hapless Confederates floundered in the ditch, the Federals began firing. "Our guns opened upon the men in the ditch with triple rounds of canister," Burnside reported, "and our infantry shot or knocked back all those whose heads appeared above the parapet." A Confederate gave his view of the hell they endured: "The enemy [was] firing artillery and musketry from all points of their works, throwing hand grenades, billets of wood, axes, &c., over the parapet into the ditch, killing and mangling our men.... Those that succeeded in climbing up the parapet to the crest were shot down, and rolling back dragged all below them back into the ditch." Burnside reported, "Most of those who reached the ditch were killed or mortally wounded.... The ground between the fort and the crest was strewed with the dead and wounded." After forty minutes of ferocious fighting against all odds, the Confederates were compelled to retire.

The failure stunned Alexander, who later severely criticized Longstreet's handling of the whole affair. The surprise attack, he charged, "was carefully arranged not to be a surprise at all. The capture of their rifle pits, at 11 P.M., naturally put the enemy's whole army on guard all night, & the presence of our assaulting brigades so close to their works all night could not be concealed. And lastly the cannon shots before dawn, as a signal to our brigades which had to advance, were equally signals to the enemy in the trenches to be ready to repel." In addition, Longstreet's "tactical formation was merely three brigades abreast in line of battle—just what it would have been in attacking a force in a wheat field!"

Longstreet had delayed and mismanaged the assault to the point of failure. Now he determined to lay siege to the town. He abruptly changed his mind, however, upon receiving news that Bragg had been defeated at Chattanooga and Federal reinforcements were headed to Burnside's aid.

6
CONCLUSION

Longstreet had bungled the entire operation. Some historians believe this was the least productive campaign ever mounted by the Confederates. One biography of Longstreet states that he made a "dull and useless campaign," and a participant in the expedition agreed. While advancing toward Knoxville, an opportunity arose to attack the Federals. "It was here that my suspicions were aroused as to the real intentions of General Longstreet," wrote General McLaws. After Longstreet had wasted six hours threatening their flank, the enemy had retreated. "I therefore concluded," wrote McLaws in an undated letter, "that he did not intend 'to make sudden Blows,' and 'rapid Movements' were not in his programme." "The soldiers," Mary Chesnut confided to her diary, "call him Peter the Slow."

Longstreet naturally tried to blame others for his failure. He relieved division commander McLaws for allegedly exhibiting a lack of confidence in the plans and efforts of himself as superior officer. (One wonders if Longstreet saw the parallel between this and his own behavior under Bragg.) Since all of Longstreet's schemes had failed, McLaws believed "my want of confidence in the plans & efforts of the commanding general, was rather complimentary than otherwise. The truth is," he continued, "Genl L. has failed in his campaign, and thought to divert attention from his great want of capacity by charging me with the neglect of some minor details." Longstreet's chief of staff again glossed over his commander's failures, explaining that he does not give their movements in detail due to "their character generally not being of the highest credit to us in rapidity or co-operation of our several commands."

Mary Boykin Chesnut: born South Carolina 1823, the first child of Mary Boykin and Stephen Decatur Miller, a governor of South Carolina and a U. S. senator; Mary's formal education ended with her father's death in 1838, but she read voraciously all her life; in 1840 she married James Chesnut, Jr., son of one of the largest land and slaveowners in the state; the Chesnuts had no children; elected to the U.S. Senate in 1858, James took Mary to Washington where she formed many friendships; after secession, James resigned his Senate seat and went to Montgomery as delegate to the Confederate Provisional Congress; there Mary's hotel quarters became the first of her remarkable wartime salons; she also began to candidly record in a private diary what she saw and heard; seven volumes of her wartime journals survive, covering most of 1861 and three months in 1865; as a close friend of Varina Davis, Mary became an ardent supporter of the president; in April 1861 she recorded the attack on Fort Sumter from a rooftop; frustrated at her woman's role as mere observer, she urged her husband to accept appointment as President Davis's aide; Mary found lodgings near the White House of the Confederacy and constantly filled the Chesnut's home with people seeking patronage, support, and respite from the war; she recorded everything in her journals; in 1864 the Chesnuts returned to South

A DIARY FROM
DIXIE, *as written by*
MARY BOYKIN CHESNUT, *wife of* JAMES
CHESNUT, JR., *United States Senator from South
Carolina, 1859–1861, and afterward an Aide
to Jefferson Davis and a Brigadier-
General in the Confederate Army*

Edited by
Isabella D. Martin and
Myrta Lockett
Avary

In the final analysis, Longstreet had no one to blame but himself. "The care and supply of Longstreet's own troops, the question of ensuring that those troops started with adequate rations, and above all the matter of preserving the internal harmony of his command—these were definitely Longstreet's duties," concluded his biographers—duties he failed to carry out in even the most rudimentary fashion.

On December 4, the Confederates withdrew from Knoxville and settled into winter quarters between Russellville and Greenville, Tennessee. Not until the spring of 1864 did Longstreet receive orders to rejoin Lee in Virginia.

James Longstreet's Western sojourn showcased his capabilities as an independent commander, and he came off badly.

Carolina, where Mary worked at a hospital and again kept open house; in 1865 she fled to North Carolina, and following Lee's surrender, to South Carolina; she still entertained friends, but in June 1865, uncertain of the future, she quit keeping her journal; during the next twenty years, reduced to poverty, she struggled to prepare her journals for publication; when she died in Camden, South Carolina, in 1886, she left an unfinished 2,500 page manuscript; she had asked a young friend, Isabella Martin, to take responsibility for her journals; in 1905 D. Appleton published *A Diary from Dixie*, edited by Isabella Martin and Myra Lockett Avary, containing less than half of Chesnut's manuscript; in 1947 another edition appeared, edited by novelist Ben Ames Williams, who also cut out much material and "smoothed up" Chesnut's prose; neither edition "made clear that the manuscript was in fact a much expanded, changed, and thoroughly restructured version of the original journal"; not until the publication in 1981 of *Mary Chesnut's Civil War*, edited by C. Vann Woodward, was Chesnut's fully revised account made available; *The Private Mary Chesnut: The Unpublished Civil War Diaries,* edited by C. Vann Woodward and Elisabeth Muhlenfeld, was published in 1984. In her writing, Chesnut presents what her biographer describes as "a panorama of her times,…a richly textured view of the concerns of women.…She loathed slavery…, but she viewed blacks through the racist lens of her time and place. Admiring the Southern woman as noble, she nevertheless linked the plight of women to that of slaves. Gifted with wit, an ironic eye, a passionate intellect and heart, and objectivity about her own shortcomings and those of her world, Chesnut provides us a stunning eyewitness account of the society that was the Confederacy."

After the lucky break at Chickamauga that allowed his troops to hit the enemy lines at the precise point where a gap had just been created, Longstreet had no successes whatever. He failed to maintain the disruption of the Federal Cracker Line; he botched an attempt to recoup its loss and blundered his way through East Tennessee. Comparing what he had heard of Longstreet with what he observed first hand, Bragg concluded that Longstreet had been greatly overrated. General Arthur M. Manigault, with fine understatement, summed up Longstreet's Western career by pointing out that although in Virginia "Longstreet's reputation stood very high, I do not think that the impression he made in the west was a very favorable one." McLaws considered Longstreet "a humbug, a man of small capacity, very obstinate, not at all chivalrous, exceedingly conceited, and totally selfish."

There is agreement among military historians that there are certain traits that a competent commander must possess: high intelligence, intuition, determination, and moral courage. A successful commander must also be able to coordinate operations.

Longstreet never exhibited signs of a superior intelligence, nor did his power to intuit appear overwhelming. His failure to prevent the Federals from opening a new supply line into Chattanooga highlights his inability to reason out and foresee the consequences of his own laziness and disobedience of orders. His determination faltered, as exemplified in his disastrous decisions during the Battle of Wauhatchie and at Knoxville. Again, at both Chattanooga and during the operations at Knoxville, Longstreet displayed his lack of moral courage by trying to blame others when his own failures led to defeat. The entire campaign through East Tennessee demonstrated his inability to coordinate an offensive.

Longstreet traveled to the West believing he alone had the ability to turn the situation in favor of the Confederacy. But he was wrong. In the West, despite his delusions of competence, Longstreet proved himself incapable of independent command. His incompetence was exceeded only by his arrogance.

Note: The Tables of Organization presented in Appendices A and B are taken from *War of the Rebellion: Official Records of the Union and Confederate Armies,* Series I, Volume 30, Part 1, pages 40–47; Part 2, pages 552–556; Part 2, pages 11–20; Series I, Volume 31, Part 1, pages 451–454. Republished by The National Historical Society, 1972.

APPENDIX A

ORGANIZATION OF THE ARMY OF THE CUMBERLAND

COMMANDER

Maj. Gen. William S. Rosecrans

GENERAL HEADQUARTERS

1st Battalion Ohio Sharpshooters, Capt. Gershom M. Barber
10th Ohio Infantry, Lieut. Col. William M. Ward
15th Pennsylvania Cavalry, Col. William J. Palmer

FOURTEENTH ARMY CORPS

Maj. Gen. George H. Thomas

GENERAL HEADQUARTERS

PROVOST GUARD

9th Michigan Infantry,[1] Col. John G. Parkhurst

ESCORT

1st Ohio Cavalry, Company L. Capt. John D. Barker

FIRST DIVISION

Brig. Gen. Absalom Baird

First Brigade

Col. Benjamin F. Scribner

38th Indiana, Lieut. Col. Daniel F. Griffin
2d Ohio, Lieut. Col. Obadiah C. Maxwell, Maj. William T. Beatty,
Capt. James Warnock
33d Ohio, Col. Oscar F. Moore

---

[1] Not engaged; guarding trains and performing provost duty.

94th Ohio, Maj. Rue P. Hutchins

10th Wisconsin, Lieut. Col. John H. Ely, Capt. Jacob W. Roby

Second Brigade
BRIG. GEN. JOHN C. STARKWEATHER

24th Illinois, Col. Geza Mihalotzy, Capt. August Mauff

79th Pennsylvania, Col. Henry A. Hambright

1st Wisconsin, Lieut. Col. George B. Bingham

21st Wisconsin, Lieut. Col. Harrison C. Hobart,
Capt. Charles H. Walker

Third Brigade[2]
BRIG. GEN. JOHN H. KING

15th United States, 1st Battalion, Capt. Albert B. Dod

16th United States, 1st Battalion, Maj. Sidney Coolidge,
Capt. R.E.A. Crofton

18th United States, 1st Battalion, Capt. George W. Smith

18th United States, 2d Battalion, Capt. Henry Haymond

19th United States, 1st Battalion, Maj. Samuel K. Dawson,
Capt. Edmund L. Smith

Artillery

Indiana Light, 4th Battery (2d Brigade), Lieut. David Flansburg,
Lieut. Henry J. Willits

1st Michigan Light, Battery A (1st Brigade),
Lieut. George W. Van Pelt, Lieut. Almerick W. Wilbur

5th United States, Battery H (3d Brigade),
Lieut. Howard M. Burnham, Lieut. Joshua A. Fessenden

SECOND DIVISION
MAJ. GEN. JAMES S. NEGLEY

First Brigade
BRIG. GEN. JOHN BEATTY

104th Illinois, Lieut. Col. Douglas Hapeman

42d Indiana, Lieut. Col. William T.B. McIntire

88th Indiana, Col. George Humphrey

15th Kentucky, Col. Marion C. Taylor

[2] For composition of the battalions, see return of casualties, p 171.

Second Brigade
Col. Timothy R. Stanley

Col. William L. Stoughton

19th Illinois, Lieut. Col. Alexander W. Raffen

11th Michigan, Col. William L. Stoughton, Lieut. Col. Melvin Mudge

18th Ohio, Lieut. Col. Charles H. Grosvenor

Third Brigade
Col. William Sirwell

37th Indiana, Lieut. Col. William D. Ward

21st Ohio, Lieut. Col. Dwella M. Stoughton, Maj. Arnold McMahan,
Capt. Charles H. Vantine

74th Ohio, Capt. Joseph Fisher

78th Pennsylvania, Lieut. Col. Archibald Blakeley

Artillery
Illinois Light, Bridges' Battery (1st Brigade), Capt. Lyman Bridges

1st Ohio Light, Battery G (3d Brigade), Capt. Alexander Marshall

1st Ohio Light, Battery M (2d Brigade), Capt. Frederick Schultz

THIRD DIVISION
Brig. Gen. John M. Brannan

First Brigade
Col. John M. Connell

82d Indiana, Col. Morton C. Hunter

17th Ohio, Lieut. Col. Durbin Ward

31st Ohio, Lieut. Col. Frederick W. Lister

38th Ohio,[3] Col. Edward H. Phelps

Second Brigade
Col. John T. Croxton

Col. William H. Hays

10th Indiana, Col. William B. Carroll, Lieut. Col. Marsh B. Taylor

74th Indiana, Col. Charles W. Chapman, Lieut. Col. Myron Baker

4th Kentucky, Lieut. Col. P. Burgess Hunt, Maj. Robert M. Kelly

10th Kentucky, Col. William H. Hays, Lieut. Col. Gabriel C. Wharton

14th Ohio, Lieut. Col. Henry D. Kingsbury

[3] Not engaged: train guard.

Third Brigade
COL. FERDINAND VAN DERVEER

87th Indiana, Col. Newell Gleason

2d Minnesota, Col. James George

9th Ohio, Col. Gustave Kammerling

35th Ohio, Lieut. Col. Henry V.N. Boynton

Artillery
1st Michigan Light, Battery D (1st Brigade), Capt. Josiah W. Church

1st Ohio Light , Battery C (2d Brigade), Lieut. Marco B. Gary

4th United States, Battery I (3d Brigade), Lieut. Frank G. Smith

FOURTH DIVISION
MAJ. GEN. JOSEPH J. REYNOLDS

First Brigade.[4]
COL. JOHN T. WILDER

92d Illinois, Col. Smith D. Atkins

98th Illinois, Col. John J. Funkhouser, Lieut. Col. Edward Kitchell

123d Illinois, Col. James Monroe

17th Indiana, Maj. William T. Jones

72d Indiana, Col. Abram O. Miller

Second Brigade
Col. Edward A. King

Col. Milton S. Robinson

68th Indiana, Capt. Harvey J. Espy

75th Indiana, Col. Milton S. Robinson, Lieut. Col. William O'Brien

101st Indiana, Lieut. Col. Thomas Doan

105th Ohio, Maj. George T. Perkins

Third Brigade
BRIG. GEN. JOHN B. TURCHIN

18th Kentucky, Lieut. Col. Hubbard K. Milward,

Capt. John B. Heltemes

11th Ohio, Col. Philander P. Lane

36th Ohio, Col. William G. Jones, Lieut. Col. Hiram F. Devol

92d Ohio, Col. Benjamin D. Fearing, Lieut. Col. Douglas Putnam, Jr.

[4] Detached from its division and serving as mounted infantry.

Artillery

Indiana Light, 18th Battery (1st Brigade), Capt. Eli Lilly

Indiana Light, 19th Battery (2d Brigade), Capt. Samuel J. Harris,
Lieut. Robert S. Lackey

Indiana Light, 21st Battery (3d Brigade), Capt. William W. Andrew

TWENTIETH ARMY CORPS
MAJ. GEN. ALEXANDER McD. McCOOK

GENERAL HEADQUARTERS
PROVOST GUARD

81st Indiana Infantry, Company H, Capt. William J. Richards

Escort—2d Kentucky Cavalry, Company I, Lieut. George W.L. Batman

FIRST DIVISION
BRIG. GEN. JEFFERSON C. DAVIS

First Brigade[5]
COL. P. SIDNEY POST

59th Illinois, Lieut. Col. Joshua C. Winters

74th Illinois, Col. Jason Marsh

75th Illinois, Col. John E. Bennett

22d Indiana, Col. Michael Gooding

Wisconsin Light Artillery, 5th Battery, Capt. George Q. Gardner

Second Brigade
BRIG. GEN. WILLIAM P. CARLIN

21st Illinois, Col. John W.S. Alexander, Capt. Chester K. Knight

38th Illinois, Lieut. Col. Daniel H. Gilmer, Capt. Willis G. Whitehurst

81st Indiana, Capt. Nevil B. Boone, Maj. James E. Calloway

101st Ohio, Lieut. Col. John Messer, Maj. Bedan B. McDanald,
Capt. Leonard D. Smith

Minnesota Light Artillery, 2d Battery, Lieut. Albert Woodbury,
Lieut. Richard L. Dawley

Third Brigade
COL. HANS C. HEG
COL. JOHN A. MARTIN

25th Illinois, Maj. Samuel D. Wall, Capt. Wesford Taggart

35th Illinois, Lieut. Col. William P. Chandler

[5] Not engaged; guarding supply train.

8th Kansas, Col. John A. Martin, Lieut. Col. James L. Abernathy

15th Wisconsin, Lieut. Col. Ole C. Johnson

Wisconsin Light Artillery, 8th Battery, Lieut. John D. McLean

SECOND DIVISION
Brig. Gen. Richard W. Johnson

First Brigade

Brig. Gen. August Willich

89th Illinois, Lieut. Col. Duncan J. Hall, Maj. William D. Williams

32nd Indiana, Lieut. Col. Frank Erdelmeyer

39th Indiana,[6] Col. Thomas J. Harrison

15th Ohio, Lieut. Col. Frank Askew

49th Ohio, Maj. Samuel F. Gray, Capt. Luther M. Strong

1st Ohio Light Artillery, Battery A, Capt. Wilbur F. Goodspeed

Second Brigade

Col. Joseph B. Dodge

79th Illinois, Col. Allen Buckner

29th Indiana, Lieut. Col. David M. Dunn

30th Indiana, Lieut. Col. Orrin D. Hurd

77th Pennsylvania, Col. Thomas E. Rose, Capt. Joseph J. Lawson

Ohio Light Artillery, 20th Battery, Capt. Edward Grosskopff

Third Brigade

Col. Philemon P. Baldwin

Col. William W. Berry

6th Indiana, Lieut. Col. Hagerman Tripp, Maj. Calvin D. Campbell

5th Kentucky, Col. William W. Berry, Capt. John M. Huston

1st Ohio, Lieut. Col. Bassett Langdon

93d Ohio, Col. Hiram Strong, Lieut. Col. William H. Martin

Indiana Light Artillery, 5th Battery, Capt. Peter Simonson

THIRD DIVISION
Maj. Gen. Philip H. Sheridan

First Brigade

Brig. Gen. William H. Lytle

Col. Silas Miller

36th Illinois, Col. Silas Miller, Lieut. Col. Porter C. Olson

[6] Detached from its Brigade and serving as mounted infantry.

88th Illinois, Lieut. Col. Alexander S. Chadbourne

21st Michigan, Col. William B. McCreery, Maj. Seymour Chase

24th Wisconsin, Lieut. Col. Theodore S. West,

Maj. Carl von Baumbach

Indiana Light Artillery, 11th Battery, Capt. Arnold Sutermeister

Second Brigade

COL. BERNARD LAIBOLDT

44th Illinois, Col. Wallace W. Barrett

73d Illinois, Col. James F. Jaquess

2d Missouri, Maj. Arnold Beck

15th Missouri, Col. Joseph Conrad

1st Missouri Light Artillery, Battery G,[7] Lieut. Gustavus Schueler

Third Brigade

COL. LUTHER P. BRADLEY

COL. NATHAN H. WALWORTH

22d Illinois, Lieut. Col. Francis Swanwick

27th Illinois, Col. Jonathan R. Miles

42d Illinois, Col. Nathan H. Walworth, Lieut. Col. John A. Hottenstein

51st Illinois, Lieut. Col. Samuel B. Raymond

1st Illinois Light Artillery, Battery C, Capt. Mark H. Prescott

TWENTY-FIRST ARMY CORPS

MAJ. GEN. THOMAS L. CRITTENDEN

GENERAL HEADQUARTERS

ESCORT

15th Illinois Cavalry, Company K, Capt. Samuel B. Sherer

FIRST DIVISION

BRIG. GEN. THOMAS J. WOOD

First Brigade

COL. GEORGE P. BUELL

100th Illinois, Col. Frederick A. Bartleson,

Maj. Charles M. Hammond

58th Indiana, Lieut. Col. James T. Embree

---

[7] Capt. Henry Hescock, chief of division artillery.

13th Michigan, Col. Joshua B. Culver, Maj. Willard G. Eaton

26th Ohio, Lieut. Col. William H. Young

Second Brigade.[8]

BRIG. GEN. GEORGE D. WAGNER

15th Indiana, Col. Gustavus A. Wood

40th Indiana, Col. John W. Blake

57th Indiana, Lieut. Col. George W. Lennard

97th Ohio, Lieut. Col. Milton Barnes

Third Brigade

COL. CHARLES G. HARKER

3d Kentucky, Col. Henry C. Dunlap

64th Ohio, Col. Alexander McIlvain

65th Ohio, Lieut. Col. Horatio N. Whitbeck, Maj. Samuel C. Brown, Capt. Thomas Powell

125th Ohio, Col. Emerson Opdycke

Artillery

Indiana Light, 8th Battery (1st Brigade), Capt. George Estep

Indiana Light, 10th Battery[9] (2d Brigade), Lieut. William A. Naylor

Ohio Light, 6th Battery (3d Brigade), Capt. Cullen Bradley

SECOND DIVISION

MAJ. GEN. JOHN M. PALMER

First Brigade

BRIG. GEN. CHARLES CRUFT

31st Indiana, Col. John T. Smith

1st Kentucky,[10] Lieut. Col. Alva R. Hadlock

2d Kentucky, Col. Thomas D. Sedgewick

90th Ohio, Col. Charles H. Rippey

Second Brigade

BRIG. GEN. WILLIAM B. HAZEN

9th Indiana, Col. Isaac C.B. Suman

6th Kentucky, Col. George T. Shackelford, Lieut. Col. Richard Rockingham, Maj. Richard T. Whitaker

41st Ohio, Col. Aquila Wiley

124th Ohio, Col. Oliver H. Payne, Maj. James B. Hampson

[8] Stationed at Chattanooga, and not engaged.

[9] Stationed at Chattanooga, and not engaged.

[10] Five companies detached as wagon guard..

Third Brigade

COL. WILLIAM GROSE

84th Illinois, Col. Louis H. Waters

36th Indiana, Lieut. Col. Oliver H.P. Carey, Maj. Gilbert Trusler

23d Kentucky, Lieut. Col. James C. Foy

6th Ohio, Col. Nicholas L. Anderson, Maj. Samuel C. Erwin

24th Ohio, Col. David J. Higgins

Artillery

CAPT. WILLIAM E. STANDART

1st Ohio Light, Battery B (1st Brigade), Lieut. Norman A. Baldwin

1st Ohio Light, Battery F (2d Brigade), Lieut. Giles J. Cockerill

4th United States, Battery H (3d Brigade), Lieut. Harry C. Cushing

4th United States, Battery M (3d Brigade),

Lieut. Francis L.D. Russell

Unattached

110th Illinois (battalion),[11] Capt. E. Hibbard Topping

THIRD DIVISION

BRIG. GEN. HORATIO P. VAN CLEVE

First Brigade

BRIG. GEN. SAMUEL BEATTY

79th Indiana, Col. Frederick Knefler

9th Kentucky, Col. George H. Cram

17th Kentucky, Col. Alexander M. Stout

19th Ohio, Lieut. Col. Henry G. Stratton

Second Brigade

COL. GEORGE F. DICK

44th Indiana, Lieut. Col. Simeon C. Aldrich

86th Indiana, Maj. Jacob C. Dick

13th Ohio, Lieut. Col. Elhannon M. Mast, Capt. Horatio G. Cosgrove

59th Ohio, Lieut. Col. Granville A. Frambes

Third Brigade

COL. SIDNEY M. BARNES

35th Indiana, Maj. John P. Dufficy

8th Kentucky, Lieut. Col. James D. Mayhew, Maj. John S. Clark

[11] Not engaged.

21st Kentucky,[12] Col. S. Woodson Price
51st Ohio, Col. Richard W. McClain, Lieut. Col. Charles H. Wood
99th Ohio, Col. Peter T. Swaine

Artillery

Indiana Light, 7th Battery, Capt. George R. Swallow
Pennsylvania Light, 26th Battery, Capt. Alanson J. Stevens,
Lieut. Samuel M. McDowell
Wisconsin Light, 3d Battery, Lieut. Cortland Livingston

RESERVE CORPS
MAJ. GEN. GORDON GRANGER

FIRST DIVISION
BRIG. GEN. JAMES B. STEEDMAN

First Brigade
BRIG. GEN. WALTER C. WHITAKER

96th Illinois, Col. Thomas E. Champion
115th Illinois, Col. Jesse H. Moore
84th Indiana, Col. Nelson Trusler
22d Michigan,[13] Col. Heber Le Favour, Lieut. Col. William Sanborn,
Capt. Alonzo M. Keeler
40th Ohio, Lieut. Col. William Jones
89th Ohio,[14] Col. Caleb H. Carlton, Capt. Isaac C. Nelson
Ohio Light Artillery, 18th Battery, Capt. Charles C. Aleshire

Second Brigade
COL. JOHN G. MITCHELL

78th Illinois, Lieut. Col. Carter Van Vleck, Lieut. George Green
98th Ohio, Capt. Moses J. Urquhart, Capt. Armstrong J. Thomas
113th Ohio, Lieut. Col. Darius B. Warner
121st Ohio, Lieut. Col. Henry B. Banning
1st Illinois Light Artillery, Battery M, Lieut. Thomas Burton

---

[12] Stationed at Whiteside's, and not engaged.
[13] Temporarily attached.
[14] Temporarily attached.

SECOND DIVISION

Second Brigade
COL. DANIEL MCCOOK
85th Illinois, Col. Caleb J. Dilworth
86th Illinois, Lieut. Col. David W. Magee
125th Illinois, Col. Oscar F. Harmon
52d Ohio, Maj. James T. Holmes
69th Ohio,[15] Lieut. Col. Joseph H. Brigham
2d Illinois Light Artillery, Battery I, Capt. Charles M. Barnett

CAVALRY CORPS
BRIG. GEN. ROBERT B. MITCHELL

FIRST DIVISION
COL. EDWARD M. MCCOOK

First Brigade
COL. ARCHIBALD P. CAMPBELL
2d Michigan, Maj. Leonidas S. Scranton
9th Pennsylvania, Lieut. Col. Roswell M. Russell
1st Tennessee, Lieut. Col. James P. Brownlow

Second Brigade
COL. DANIEL M. RAY
2d Indiana, Maj. Joseph B. Presdee
4th Indiana, Lieut. Col. John T. Deweese
2d Tennessee, Lieut. Col. William R. Cook
1st Wisconsin, Col. Oscar H. La Grange
1st Ohio Light Artillery, Battery D (section),
Lieut. Nathaniel M. Newell

Third Brigade
COL. LOUIS D. WATKINS
4th Kentucky, Col. Wickliffe Cooper
5th Kentucky, Lieut. Col. William T. Hoblitzell
6th Kentucky, Maj. Louis A. Gratz

[15] Temporarily attached.

SECOND DIVISION
BRIG. GEN. GEORGE CROOK

First Brigade
COL. ROBERT H.G. MINTY

3d Indiana (battalion), Lieut. Col. Robert Klein
4th Michigan, Maj. Horace Gray
7th Pennsylvania, Lieut. Col. James J. Seibert
4th United States, Capt. James B. McIntyre

Second Brigade
COL. ELI LONG

2d Kentucky, Col. Thomas P. Nicholas
1st Ohio, Lieut. Col. Valentine Cupp, Maj. Thomas J. Patten
3d Ohio, Lieut. Col. Charles B. Seidel
4th Ohio, Lieut. Col. Oliver P. Robie

Artillery

Chicago (Illinois) Board of Trade Battery, Capt. James H. Stokes

ORGANIZATION OF
THE DEPARTMENT OF THE OHIO
COMMANDER
MAJ. GEN. AMBROSE E. BURNSIDE

NINTH ARMY CORPS
BRIG. GEN. ROBERT B. POTTER[16]

HEADQUARTERS
2D U.S. ARTILLERY, BATTERY E, LIEUT. SAMUEL N. BENJAMIN

FIRST DIVISION[17]
BRIG. GEN. EDWARD FERRERO

First Brigade
COL. DAVID MORRISON

36th Massachusetts, Maj. Arthur A. Goodell
8th Michigan, Col. Frank Graves
79th New York, Lieut. Col. John More
45th Pennsylvania, Col. Francis M. Hills

[16] Commanding since August 25, *vice* Parke, "absent sick.".
[17] This division embarked at Haynes' Bluff, Mississippi, August 3; arrived at Cincinnati, Ohio, August 12, and encamped near Covington, Kentucky. On August 18, it moved to Nicholasville, and on the 26th to Crab Orchard.

Second Brigade

Col. Ebenezer W. Peirce

29th Massachusetts, Maj. Charles Chipman

27th Michigan, Col. Dorus M. Fox

46th New York, Capt. Alphons Serviere

50th Pennsylvania, Maj. Edward Overton, Jr.

Third Brigade

Maj. Cornelius Byington

2d Michigan, Capt. John V. Ruehle

17th Michigan, Capt. Lorin L. Comstock

20th Michigan, Maj. Byron M. Cutcheon

100th Pennsylvania, Maj. James H. Cline

Artillery

3d United States, Batteries L and M, Capt. John Edwards, Jr.

SECOND DIVISION[18]

Col. Simon G. Griffin

First Brigade

Col. Zenas R. Bliss

6th New Hampshire, Maj. Phin P. Bixby

9th New Hampshire, Capt. Augustus S. Edgerly

7th Rhode Island, Capt. Alfred M. Channell

Second Brigade

Lieut. Col. Edwin Schall

35th Massachusetts, Maj. Nathaniel Wales

11th New Hampshire, Capt. Hollis O. Dudley

51st New York, Lieut. Col. R. Charlton Mitchell

51st Pennsylvania, Maj. William J. Bolton

Artillery

2d New York Light, Battery L, Capt. Jacob Roemer

Pennsylvania Light, Battery D, Capt. George W. Durell

---

[18] This division embarked at Haynes' Bluff, Mississippi, August 8; arrived at Cincinnati, Ohio, August 20, and encamped near Covington, Kentucky. On August 26, it moved to Nicholasville.

TWENTY-THIRD ARMY CORPS[19]
Maj. Gen. George L. Hartsuff

FIRST DIVISION
Brig. Gen. Jeremiah T. Boyle

Bowling Green, Ky.

11th Kentucky, Capt. Eugene F. Kinnaird

26th Kentucky (seven companies), Capt. Rowland E. Hackett

8th Kentucky Cavalry (four companies), Maj. Joseph M. Kennedy

Mount Sterling, Ky.

Lieut. Col. Ralph R. Maltby

10th Kentucky Cavalry, Maj. James L. Foley

14th Kentucky Cavalry (four companies), Maj. Robert T. Williams

Munfordville, Ky.

Col. Charles D. Pennebaker

27th Kentucky, Lieut. Col. John H. Ward

33d Kentucky (four companies), Lieut. Col. James F. Lauck

6th Michigan Battery, Capt. Luther F. Hale

Camp Nelson, Ky.

21st Massachusetts, Capt. Charles W. Davis

Frankfort, Ky.

Col. Thomas B. Allard

2d Maryland, Maj. John M. Santmyer

Hopkinsville, Ky.

Col. Eli H. Murray

3d Kentucky Cavalry (eight companies), Capt. John W. Breathitt

Louisa, Ky.

Col. George W. Gallup

14th Kentucky, Lieut. Col. Orlando Brown, Jr.

39th Kentucky, Col. John Dils, Jr.

New Haven, Ky.

63d Indiana (six companies), Col. James McManomy

---

[19] As reorganized under General Orders, No. 18, corps headquarters, August 6, 1863.
See Series I, Vol XXIII, Part II, p.595.

Lexington, Ky.
COL. JOSHUA K. SIGFRIED
6th Indiana Cavalry (four companies),
Lieut. Col. Courtland C. Matson
1st Ohio Heavy Artillery (two companies), Capt. Amos B. Cole
48th Pennsylvania, Maj. Joseph A. Gilmour

Louisville, Ky.
20th Kentucky, Maj. Thomas B. Waller
34th Kentucky, Company G, Capt. Christopher C. Hare

Eminence, Ky.
9th Kentucky Cavalry, Col. Richard T. Jacob

Russellville, Ky.
COL. BENJAMIN H. BRISTOW
91st Indiana (seven companies), Lieut. Col. John Mehringer
3d Kentucky Cavalry (four companies), Maj. Lewis Wolfley
8th Kentucky Cavalry (four companies), Maj. Samuel M. Starling
22d Indiana Battery, Lieut. Edward W. Nicholson

Glasgow, Ky.
COL. WILLIAM Y. DILLARD
34th Kentucky (eight companies), Maj. Milton T. Callahan

Muldraugh's Hill, Ky.
50th Ohio, Col. Silas A. Strickland

Smithland, Ky.
15th Kentucky Cavalry, Company C, Capt. Jonathan Belt

SECOND DIVISION[20]
BRIG. GEN. JULIUS WHITE

First Brigade
COL. ORLANDO H. MOORE
80th Indiana, Lieut. Col. James L. Culbertson
16th Kentucky, Col. James W. Gault
25th Michigan, Capt. Samuel L. Demarest
118th Ohio, Col. Samuel R. Mott
Elgin (Illinois) Battery, Capt. Andrew M. Wood

[20] Near Montgomery, Tennessee General White assumed command August 21.

Second Brigade

COL. MARSHAL W. CHAPIN

107th Illinois, Col. Joseph J. Kelly

13th Kentucky, Col. William E. Hobson

23d Michigan, Lieut. Col. Oliver L. Spaulding

111th Ohio, Lieut. Col. Moses R. Brailey

Illinois Battery, Capt. Edward C. Henshaw

THIRD DIVISION[21]

BRIG. GEN. MILO S. HASCALL

First Brigade

COL. SAMUEL A. GILBERT

12th Kentucky, Col. William A. Hoskins

44th Ohio, Maj. Alpheus S. Moore

100th Ohio, Col. Patrick S. Slevin

104th Ohio, Col. James W. Reilly

1st Ohio Light Artillery, Battery D, Lieut. William H. Pease

Second Brigade

COL. DANIEL CAMERON

65th Illinois (eight companies), Lieut. Col. William S. Stewart

24th Kentucky, Col. John S. Hurt

103d Ohio, Col. John S. Casement

8th Tennessee, Col. Felix A. Reeve

Wilder (Indiana) Battery, Capt. Hubbard T. Thomas

FOURTH DIVISION

BRIG. GEN. SAMUEL P. CARTER

First Brigade

COL. ROBERT K. BYRD

112th Illinois,[22] Col. Thomas J. Henderson

8th Michigan Cavalry, Lieut. Col. Grover S. Wormer

45th Ohio,[23] Lieut. Col. George E. Ross

1st Tennessee,[24] Maj. John Ellis

15th Indiana Battery, Lieut. William H. Torr

---

[21] About Wartburg, Tennessee.

[22] Mounted infantry.

[23] Mounted infantry.

[24] Mounted infantry.

Second Brigade
COL. JOHN W. FOSTER

14th Illinois Cavalry, Col. Horace Capron
5th Indiana Cavalry, Col. Felix W. Graham
65th Indiana,[25] Lieut. Col. Thomas Johnson
9th Ohio Cavalry (four companies), Maj. William D. Hamilton
8th Tennessee Cavalry (four companies), Maj. John M. Sawyers
1st Illinois Light Artillery, Battery M, Lieut. John H. Colvin

Third Brigade
BRIG. GEN. JAMES M. SHACKELFORD

9th Michigan Cavalry, Col. James I. David
2d Ohio Cavalry, Lieut. Col. George A. Purington
7th Ohio Cavalry, Col. Israel Garrard
2d Tennessee,[26] Maj. Daniel A. Carpenter
11th Michigan Battery, Capt. Charles J. Thompson
1st Tennessee Battery, Capt. R. Clay Crawford

Unattached
Cavalry Brigade
COL. FRANK WOLFORD

1st Kentucky, Lieut. Col. Silas Adams
11th Kentucky (nine companies), Maj. Milton Graham
12th Kentucky, Col. Eugene W. Crittenden
Howitzer Battery,[27] Lieut. Jesse S. Law

Reserve Artillery
CAPT. ANDREW J. KONKLE

2d Illinois Light, Battery M, Capt. John C. Phillips
24th Indiana Battery, Lieut. Henry W. Shafer
19th Ohio Battery, Capt. Joseph C. Shields
1st Rhode Island Light, Battery D, Capt. William W. Buckley

District of Ohio
BRIG. GEN. JACOB D. COX

Camp Dennison
BRIG. GEN. MASON BRAYMAN

4th Ohio Cavalry Battalion, Maj. Joseph T. Wheeler
9th Ohio Cavalry (detachment)[28]
Ohio Sharpshooters, Ninth Company, Lieut. Aquila Coonrad
24th Ohio Battery, Capt. John L. Hill

[25] Mounted infantry.
[26] Mounted infantry.
[27] Improvised.
[28] Commander not of record.

Cincinnati

LIEUT. COL. SETH EASTMAN

115th Ohio, Companies A, B, C, E, F, H, and I,
Lieut. Col. Thomas C. Boone
Ohio Sharpshooters, Eighth Company, Capt. Charles A. Barton
21st Ohio Battery, Capt. James W. Patterson

Mason's Command

BRIG. GEN. JOHN S. MASON

88th Ohio, Col. George W. Neff (Camp Chase)
115th Ohio, Company D, Capt. Lewis McCoy
Provost Guard, two companies (Columbus), Maj. John W. Skiles

Covington, Ky.

COL. CHAUNCEY G. HAWLEY

1st Ohio Heavy Artillery (ten companies), Col. Chauncey G. Hawley
115th Ohio, Companies G and K, Lieut. Albert W. Thompson

Sandusky

Hoffman (Ohio) Battalion, Maj. William S. Pierson

District of Indiana and Michigan

BRIG. GEN. ORLANDO B. WILLCOX

63d Indiana (four companies), Maj. Henry Tindall
6th Indiana Cavalry,[29] Col. James Biddle
115th Indiana, Lieut. Col. Alfred J. Hawn
1st Indiana Heavy Artillery (one company), Lieut. Henry H. Olds
23d Indiana Battery, Capt. James H. Myers
3d Indiana Cavalry, Companies L and M, Capt. Oliver M. Powers
12th Michigan Battery, Capt. Ira G. Robertson
Exchanged and paroled prisoners, Capt. David W. Hamilton

District of Illinois

BRIG. GEN. JACOB AMMEN

16th Illinois Cavalry (five companies), Col. Christian Thielemann
65th Illinois (two companies), Capt. James S. Putnam
113th Illinois (five companies), Capt. George W. Lyman
1st Michigan Sharpshooters, Col. Charles V. De Land
9th Vermont, Company G, Lieut. William C. Holman

[29] Left for the field August 31.

APPENDIX B

ORGANIZATION OF THE ARMY OF TENNESSEE
COMMANDER
GEN. BRAXTON BRAGG

HEADQUARTERS
ESCORT

CAPT. GUY DREUX

Dreux's Company Louisiana Cavalry, Lieut. O. De Buis
Holloway's Company Alabama Cavalry, Capt. E.M. Holloway

RIGHT WING
LIEUT. GEN. LEONIDAS POLK

ESCORT

Greenleaf's Company Louisiana Cavalry, Capt. Leeds Greenleaf

CHEATHAM'S DIVISION
MAJ. GEN. BENJAMIN F. CHEATHAM[1]

ESCORT

Company G, 2d Georgia Cavalry, Capt. Thomas M. Merritt

Jackson's Brigade
BRIG. GEN. JOHN K. JACKSON

1st Georgia (Confederate), 2d Battalion, Maj. James Clarke Gordon
5th Georgia, Col. Charles P. Daniel
2d Georgia Battalion Sharpshooters, Maj. Richard H. Whiteley
5th Mississippi, Lieut. Col. W.L. Sykes, Maj. John B. Herring
8th Mississippi, Col. John C. Wilkinson

Smith's Brigade
BRIG. GEN. PRESTON SMITH
COL. ALFRED J. VAUGHAN, JR.

11th Tennessee, Col. George W. Gordon
12th Tennessee, Col. William M. Watkins
47th Tennessee, Col. William M. Watkins
13th Tennessee, Col. A.J. Vaughan, Jr., and Lieut. Col. R.W. Pitman
154th Tennessee, Col. A.J. Vaughan, Jr., and Lieut. Col. R.W. Pitman

[1] Of Polk's corps.

29th Tennessee, Col. Horace Rice

Dawson's (battalion[2]) Sharpshooters, Maj. J.W. Dawson, Maj. William Green, Maj. James Purl

Maney's Brigade
BRIG. GEN. GEORGE MANEY

1st Tennessee, Col. Hume R. Feild

27th Tennessee, Col. Hume R. Feild

4th Tennessee (Provisional Army), Col. James A. McMurry, Lieut. Col. Robert N. Lewis, Maj. Oliver A. Bradshaw, Capt. Joseph Bostick

6th Tennessee, Col. George C. Porter

9th Tennessee, Col. George C. Porter

24th Tennessee Battalion Sharpshooters, Maj. Frank Maney

Wright's Brigade
BRIG. GEN. MARCUS J. WRIGHT

8th Tennessee, Col. John H. Anderson

16th Tennessee, Col. D.M. Donnell

28th Tennessee, Col. Sidney S. Stanton

38th Tennessee, and Maj. Thomas B. Murray's (Tennessee) Battalion, Col. John C. Carter

51st Tennessee, Lieut. Col. John G. Hall

52d Tennessee, Lieut. Col. John G. Hall

Strahl's Brigade
BRIG. GEN. OTHO F. STRAHL

4th Tennessee, Col. Jonathan J. Lamb

5th Tennessee, Col. Jonathan J. Lamb

19th Tennessee, Col. Francis M. Walker

24th Tennessee, Col. John A. Wilson

31st Tennessee, Col. Egbert E. Tansil

33d Tennessee, Col. Warner P. Jones

Artillery
MAJ. MELANCTHON SMITH

Carnes' (Tennessee) Battery, Capt. William W. Carnes

Scogin's (Georgia) Battery, Capt. John Scogin

Scott's (Tennessee) Battery, Lieut. John H. Marsh, Lieut., A.T. Watson, Capt. William L. Scott

Smith's (Mississippi) Battery, Lieut. William B. Turner

Stanford's (Mississippi) Battery, Capt. Thomas J. Stanford

[2] Composed of two companies from the 11th Tennessee, two from the 12th and 47th Tennessee (consolidated), and one from the 154th Senior Tennessee.

HILL'S CORPS
LIEUT. GEN. DANIEL H. HILL

CLEBURNE'S DIVISION
MAJ. GEN. PATRICK R. CLEBURNE

ESCORT
Sanders' Company Tennessee Cavalry, Capt. C.F. Sanders

Wood's Brigade
BRIG. GEN. S.A.M. WOOD
16th Alabama, Maj. John H. McGaughy, Capt. Frederick A. Ashford
33d Alabama, Col. Samuel Adams
45th Alabama, Col. E.B. Breedlove
18th Alabama Battalion, Maj. John H. Gibson, Col. Samuel Adams[3]
32d Mississippi, Col. M.P. Lowrey
45th Mississippi, Col. M.P. Lowrey
15th Mississippi Battalion Sharpshooters, Maj. A.T. Hawkins,
Capt. Daniel Coleman

Polk's Brigade
BRIG. GEN. LUCIUS E. POLK
1st Arkansas, Col. John W. Colquitt
3d Confederate, Col. J.A. Smith
5th Confederate, Col. J.A. Smith
2d Tennessee, Col. William D. Robison
35th Tennessee, Col. Benjamin J. Hill
48th Tennessee, Col. George H. Nixon

Deshler's Brigade
BRIG. GEN. JAMES DESHLER
COL. ROGER Q. MILLS
9th Arkansas, Lieut. Col. A.S. Hutchison
24th Arkansas, Lieut. Col. A.S. Hutchison
6th Texas Infantry, Col. Roger Q. Mills and
Lieut. Col. T. Scott Anderson
10th Texas Infantry, Col. Roger Q. Mills and
Lieut. Col. T. Scott Anderson
15th Texas Infantry,[4] Col. Roger Q. Mills and
Lieut. Col. T. Scott Anderson

[3] 33d Alabama.
[4] Dismounted.

17th Texas Cavalry,[5] Col. F.C. Wilkes, Lieut. Col. John T. Coit, and
Maj. William A. Taylor

18th Texas Cavalry, Col. F.C. Wilkes, Lieut. Col. John T. Coit, and
Maj. William A. Taylor

24th Texas Cavalry, Col. F.C. Wilkes, Lieut. Col. John T. Coit, and
Maj. William A. Taylor

25th Texas Cavalry, Col. F.C. Wilkes, Lieut. Col. John T. Coit, and
Maj. William A. Taylor

Artillery
MAJ. T.R. HOTCHKISS
CAPT. HENRY C. SEMPLE

Calvert's (Arkansas) Battery, Lieut. Thomas J. Key
Douglas' (Texas) Battery, Capt. James P. Douglas
Semple's (Alabama) Battery, Capt. Henry C. Semple and
Lieut. R.W. Goldthwaite

BRECKINRIDGE'S DIVISION
MAJ. GEN. JOHN C. BRECKINRIDGE

ESCORT
Foules' Company Mississippi Cavalry, Capt. H.L. Foules

Helm's Brigade
BRIG. GEN. BENJAMIN H. HELM
COL. JOSEPH H. LEWIS

41st Alabama, Col. Martin L. Stansel
2d Kentucky, Lieut. Col. James W. Hewitt, Lieut. Col. James W. Moss
4th Kentucky, Col. Joseph P. Nuckols, Maj. Thomas W. Thompson
6th Kentucky, Col. Joseph H. Lewis, Lieut. Col. Martin H. Cofer
9th Kentucky, Col. John W. Caldwell, Lieut. Col. John C. Wickliffe

Adams' Brigade
BRIG. GEN. DANIEL W. ADAMS
COL. RANDALL L. GIBSON

32d Alabama, Maj. John C. Kimbell
13th Louisiana, Col. Randall L. Gibson, Col. Leon von Zinken, and
Capt. E.M. Dubroca
20th Louisiana, Col. Randall L. Gibson, Col. Leon von Zinken, and
Capt. E.M. Dubroca

[5] Dismounted.

16th Louisiana, Col. Daniel Gober

25th Louisiana, Col. Daniel Gober

19th Louisiana, Lieut. Col. Richard W. Turner, Maj. Loudon Butler,
Capt. H.A. Kennedy

14th Louisiana Battalion, Maj. J.E. Austin

Stovall's Brigade
BRIG. GEN. MARCELLUS A. STOVALL

1st Florida, Col. William S. Dilworth

3d Florida, Col. William S. Dilworth

4th Florida, Col. W.L.L. Bowen

47th Georgia, Capt. William S. Phillips, Capt. Joseph S. Cone

60th North Carolina, Lieut. Col. James M. Ray,
Capt. James Thomas Weaver

Artillery
MAJ. RICE E. GRAVES

Cobb's (Kentucky) Battery, Capt. Robert Cobb

Graves' (Kentucky) Battery, Lieut. S.M. Spencer

Mebane's (Tennessee) Battery, Capt. John W. Mebane

Slocomb's (Louisiana) Battery, Capt. C.H. Slocomb

RESERVE CORPS
MAJ. GEN. WILLIAM H.T. WALKER

WALKER'S DIVISION
BRIG. GEN. STATES R. GIST

Gist's Brigade
BRIG. GEN. STATES R. GIST
COL. PEYTON H. COLQUITT
LIEUT. COL. LEROY NAPIER

46th Georgia, Col. Peyton H. Colquitt, Maj. A.M. Speer

8th Georgia Battalion, Lieut. Col. Leroy Napier, Maj. Z.L. Watters

16th South Carolina,[6] Col. James McCullough

24th South Carolina, Col. Clement H. Stevens,
Lieut. Col. Ellison Capers

[6] Not engaged; at Rome.

Ector's Brigade

BRIG. GEN. MATTHEW D. ECTOR

Stone's (Alabama) Battalion Sharpshooters, Maj. T.O. Stone

Pound's (Mississippi) Battalion Sharpshooters, Capt. M. Pound

29th North Carolina, Col. William B. Creasman

9th Texas, Col. William H. Young

10th Texas Cavalry,[7] Lieut. Col. C.R. Earp

14th Texas Cavalry,[8] Col. J.L. Camp

32d Texas Cavalry,[9] Col. Julius A. Andrews

Wilson's Brigade

COL. CLAUDIUS C. WILSON

25th Georgia, Lieut. Col. A.J. Williams

29th Georgia, Lieut. George R. McRae

30th Georgia, Lieut. Col. James S. Boynton

1st Georgia Battalion Sharpshooters, Maj. Arthur Shaaff

4th Louisiana Battalion, Lieut. Col. John McEnery

Artillery

Ferguson's (South Carolina) Battery,[10] Lieut. R.T. Beauregard

Howell's (Georgia) Battery (formerly Martin's), Capt. Evan P. Howell

LIDDELL'S DIVISION

BRIG. GEN. ST. JOHN R. LIDDELL

Liddell's Brigade

COL. DANIEL C. GOVAN

2d Arkansas, Lieut. Col. Reuben F. Harvey and Capt. A.T. Meek

15th Arkansas, Lieut. Col. Reuben F. Harvey and Capt. A.T. Meek

5th Arkansas, Col. L. Featherston and Lieut. Col. John E. Murray

13th Arkansas, Col. L. Featherston and Lieut. Col. John E. Murray

6th Arkansas, Col. D.A. Gillespie and Lieut. Col. Peter Snyder

7th Arkansas, Col. D.A. Gillespie and Lieut. Col. Peter Snyder

8th Arkansas, Lieut. Col. George F. Baucum, Maj. A. Watkins

1st Louisiana (Regulars), Lieut. Col. George F. Baucum,[11]

Maj. A. Watkins[12]

[7] Serving as infantry.
[8] Serving as infantry.
[9] Serving as infantry.
[10] Not engaged; at Rome.
[11] 8th Arkansas.
[12] 8th Arkansas.

Walthall's Brigade

Brig. Gen. Edward C. Walthall

24th Mississippi, Lieut. Col. R.P. McKelvaine, Maj. W.C. Staples,
Capt. B.F. Toomer, Capt. J.D. Smith

27th Mississippi, Col. James A. Campbell

29th Mississippi, Col. William F. Brantly

30th Mississippi, Col. Junius I. Scales, Lieut. Col. Hugh A. Reynolds,
Maj. James M. Johnson

34th Mississippi, Maj. William G. Pegram, Capt. H.J. Bowen, Lieut.
Col. Hugh A. Reynolds[13]

Artillery

Capt. Charles Swett

Fowler's (Alabama) Battery, Capt. William H. Fowler

Warren Light Artillery (Mississippi Battery), Lieut. H. Shannon

LEFT WING

Lieut. Gen. James Longstreet

HINDMAN'S DIVISION[14]

Maj. Gen. Thomas C. Hindman

Brig. Gen. Patton Anderson

ESCORT

Lenoir's Company Alabama Cavalry, Capt. T.M. Lenoir

Anderson's Brigade

Brig. Gen. Patton Anderson

Col. J.H. Sharp

7th Mississippi, Col. W.H. Bishop

9th Mississippi, Maj. T.H. Lynam

10th Mississippi, Lieut. Col. James Barr

41st Mississippi, Col. W.F. Tucker

44th Mississippi, Col. J.H. Sharp, Lieut. Col. R.G. Kelsey

9th Mississippi Battalion Sharpshooters, Maj. W.C. Richards

Garrity's (Alabama) Battery, Capt. James Garrity

[13] 30th Mississippi.
[14] Of Polk's corps.

Deas' Brigade

BRIG. GEN. ZACH. C. DEAS

19th Alabama, Col. Samuel K. McSpadden
22nd Alabama, Lieut. Col. John Weedon, Capt. Harry T. Toulmin
25th Alabama, Col. George D. Johnston
39th Alabama, Col. Whitfield Clark
50th Alabama, Col. J.G. Coltart
17th Alabama Battalion Sharpshooters, Capt. James F. Nabers
Dent's (Alabama) Battery (formerly Robertson's), Capt. S.H. Dent

Manigault's Brigade

BRIG. GEN. ARTHUR M. MANIGAULT

24th Alabama, Col. N.N. Davis
28th Alabama, Col. John C. Reid
34th Alabama, Maj. John N. Slaughter
10th South Carolina, Col. James F. Pressley
19th South Carolina, Col. James F. Pressley
Waters' (Alabama) Battery, Lieut. Charles W. Watkins

BUCKNER'S CORPS
MAJ. GEN. SIMON B. BUCKNER

ESCORT
Clark's Company Tennessee Cavalry, Capt. J.W. Clark

STEWART'S DIVISION
MAJ. GEN. ALEXANDER P. STEWART

Johnson's Brigade[15]

BRIG. GEN. BUSHROD R. JOHNSON

COL. JOHN S. FULTON

17th Tennessee, Lieut. Col. Watt W. Floyd
23d Tennessee, Col. R.H. Keeble
25th Tennessee, Lieut. Col. R.B. Snowden
44th Tennessee, Lieut. Col. John L. McEwen, Jr., Maj. G.M. Crawford

Bate's Brigade

BRIG. GEN. WILLIAM B. BATE

58th Alabama, Col. Bushrod Jones
37th Georgia, Col. A.F. Rudler, Lieut. Col. Joseph T. Smith

[15] Part of Johnson's provisional division.

4th Georgia Battalion Sharpshooters, Maj. T.D. Caswell,
Capt. B.M. Turner, Lieut. Joel Towers
15th Tennessee, Col. R.C. Tyler, Lieut. Col. R. Dudley Frayser, and
Capt. R.M. Tankesley
37th Tennessee, Col. R.C. Tyler, Lieut. Col. R. Dudley Frayser, and
Capt. R.M. Tankesley
20th Tennessee, Col. Thomas B. Smith, Maj. W.M. Shy

Brown's Brigade
BRIG. GEN. JOHN C. BROWN
COL. EDMUND C. COOK

18th Tennessee, Col. Joseph B. Palmer, Lieut. Col. William R. Butler,
Capt. Gideon H. Lowe
26th Tennessee, Col. John M. Lillard, Maj. Richard M. Saffell
32d Tennessee, Col. Edmund C. Cook, Capt. Calaway G. Tucker
45th Tennessee, Col. Anderson Searcy
23d Tennessee Battalion, Maj. Tazewell W. Newman,
Capt. W.P. Simpson

Clayton's Brigade
BRIG. GEN. HENRY D. CLAYTON

18th Alabama, Col. J.T. Holtzclaw, Lieut. Col. R.F. Inge,
Maj. P.F. Hunley
36th Alabama, Col. Lewis T. Woodruff
38th Alabama, Lieut. Col. A.R. Lankford

Artillery
MAJ. J. WESLEY ELDRIDGE

1st Arkansas Battery, Capt. John T. Humphreys
T.H. Dawson's (Georgia) Battery, Lieut. R.W. Anderson
Eufaula Artillery (Alabama Battery), Capt. McDonald Oliver
Company E, 9th Georgia Artillery Battalion (Billington W. York's
Battery), Lieut. William S. Everett

PRESTON'S DIVISION
BRIG. GEN. WILLIAM PRESTON

Gracie's Brigade

BRIG. GEN. ARCHIBALD GRACIE, JR.

43d Alabama, Col. Young M. Moody

1st Alabama Battalion,[16] Lieut. Col. John H. Holt,

Capt. George W. Huguley

2d Alabama Battalion,[17] Lieut. Col. Bolling Hall, Jr.,

Capt. W.D. Walden

3d Alabama Battalion,[18] Lieut. Col. John W.A. Sanford

4th Alabama Battalion,[19] Maj. John D. McLennan

63d Tennessee, Lieut. Col. Abraham Fulkerson, Maj. John A. Aiken

Trigg's Brigade

COL. ROBERT C. TRIGG

1st Florida Cavalry,[20] Col. G. Troup Maxwell

6th Florida, Col. J.J. Finley

7th Florida, Col. Robert Bullock

54th Virginia, Lieut. Col. John J. Wade

Third Brigade

COL. JOHN H. KELLY

65th Georgia, Col. R.H. Moore

5th Kentucky, Col. Hiram Hawkins

58th North Carolina, Col. John B. Palmer

63d Virginia, Maj. James M. French

Artillery Battalion

MAJ. A. LEYDEN

Jeffress' (Virginia) Battery, Captain William C. Jeffress

Peeples' (Georgia) Battery, Capt. Tyler M. Peeples

Wolihin's (Georgia) Battery, Capt. Andrew M. Wolihin

Reserve Corps Artillery

MAJ. SAMUEL C. WILLIAMS

Baxter's (Tennessee) Battery, Capt. Edmund D. Baxter

Darden's (Mississippi) Battery, Capt. Putnam Darden

Kolb's (Alabama) Battery, Capt. R.F. Kolb

McCants' (Florida) Battery, Capt. Robert P. McCants

---

[16] Hilliard's Legion.
[17] Hilliard's Legion.
[18] Hilliard's Legion.
[19] Artillery battalion, Hilliard's Legion, serving as infantry.
[20] Dismounted.

JOHNSON'S DIVISION[21]
BRIG. GEN. BUSHROD R. JOHNSON

Gregg's Brigade
BRIG. GEN. JOHN GREGG
COL. CYRUS A. SUGG

3d Tennessee, Col. Calvin H. Walker

10th Tennessee, Col. William Grace

30th Tennessee, Lieut. Col. James J. Turner,
Capt. Charles S. Douglass

41st Tennessee, Lieut. Col. James D. Tillman

50th Tennessee, Col. Cyrus A. Sugg,
Lieut. Col. Thomas W. Beaumont, Maj. Christopher W. Robertson,
Col. Calvin H. Walker[22]

1st Tennessee Battalion, Maj. Stephen H. Colms,
Maj. Christopher W. Robertson[23]

7th Texas, Col. H.B. Granbury, Maj. K.M. Vanzandt

Bledsoe's (Missouri) Battery, Lieut. R.L. Wood

McNair's Brigade
BRIG. GEN. EVANDER MCNAIR
COL. DAVID COLEMAN

1st Arkansas Mounted Rifles,[24] Col. Robert W. Harper

2d Arkansas Mounted Rifles,[25] Col. James A. Williamson

25th Arkansas, Lieut. Col. Eli Hufstedler

4th and 31st Arkansas and 4th Arkansas Battalion (consolidated),
Maj. J.A. Ross

39th North Carolina, Col. David Coleman

Culpeper's (South Carolina) Battery, Capt. James F. Culpeper

LONGSTREET'S CORPS[26]
MAJ. GEN. JOHN B. HOOD

McLAW'S DIVISION
BRIG. GEN. JOSEPH B. KERSHAW
MAJ. GEN. LAFAYETTE MCLAWS

---

[21] A Provisional organization, embracing Johnson's and part of the time Robertson's brigades, as well as Gregg's and McNair's. September 19 attached to Longstreet's corps, under Major-General Hood.

[22] 3d Tennessee.

[23] 50th Tennessee.

[24] Dismounted.

[25] Dismounted.

[26] Army of Northern Virginia. Organization taken from return of that army for August 31, 1863. Pickett's division was left in Virginia.

Kershaw's Brigade

BRIG. GEN. JOSEPH B. KERSHAW

2d South Carolina, Lieut. Col. Franklin Gaillard

3d South Carolina, Col. James D. Nance

7th South Carolina, Lieut. Col. Elbert Bland, Maj. John S. Hard,

Capt. E.J. Goggans

8th South Carolina, Col. John W. Henagan

15th South Carolina, Col. Joseph F. Gist

3d South Carolina Battalion, Capt. Joshua M. Townsend

Humphreys' Brigade

BRIG. GEN. BENJAMIN G. HUMPHREYS

13th Mississippi, Lieut. Col. Kennon McElroy

17th Mississippi, Lieut. Col. John C. Fiser

18th Mississippi, Capt. W.F. Hubbard

21st Mississippi, Lieut. Col. D.N. Moody

Wofford's Brigade[27]

BRIG. GEN. WILLIAM T. WOFFORD

16th Georgia

18th Georgia

24th Georgia

3d Georgia Battalion Sharpshooters

Cobb's (Georgia) Legion

Phillips (Georgia) Legion

Bryan's Brigade[28]

BRIG. GEN. GOODE BRYAN

10th Georgia

50th Georgia

51st Georgia

53d Georgia

HOOD'S DIVISION
MAJ. GEN. JOHN B. HOOD
BRIG. GEN. E. MCIVER LAW

---

[27] Longstreet's report indicates that these brigades did not arrive in time to take part in the battle.
[28] Longstreet's report indicates that these brigades did not arrive in time to take part in the battle.

Jenkins' Brigade[29]

BRIG. GEN. MICAH JENKINS

1st South Carolina

2d South Carolina Rifles

5th South Carolina

6th South Carolina

Hampton Legion

Palmetto Sharpshooters

Law's Brigade

BRIG. GEN. E. MCIVER LAW

COL. JAMES L. SHEFFIELD

4th Alabama, Col. Pinckney D. Bowles

15th Alabama, Col. W.C. Oates

44th Alabama, Col. William F. Perry

47th Alabama, Maj. James M. Campbell

48th Alabama, Lieut. Col. William M. Hardwick

Robertson's Brigade[30]

BRIG. GEN. JEROME B. ROBERTSON

COL. VAN H. MANNING

3d Arkansas, Col. Van H. Manning

1st Texas, Capt. R.J. Harding

4th Texas, Lieut. Col. John P. Bane, Capt. R.H. Bassett

5th Texas, Maj. J.C. Rogers, Capt. J.S. Cleveland, Capt. T.T. Clay

Anderson's Brigade[31]

BRIG. GEN. GEORGE T. ANDERSON

7th Georgia

8th Georgia

9th Georgia

11th Georgia

59th Georgia

Benning's Brigade

BRIG. GEN. HENRY L. BENNING

2d Georgia, Lieut. Col. William S. Shepherd, Maj. W.W. Charlton

15th Georgia, Col. Dudley M. DuBose, Maj. P.J. Shannon

17th Georgia, Lieut. Col. Charles W. Matthews

20th Georgia, Col. J.D. Waddell

[29] Did not arrive in time to take part in the battle. Jenkins' brigade assigned to the division September 11, 1863.

[30] Served part of the time in Johnson's provisional division.

[31] Did not arrive in time to take part in the battle. Jenkins' brigade assigned to the division September 11, 1863.

Corps Artillery[32]
COL. E. PORTER ALEXANDER

Fickling's (South Carolina) Battery

Jordan's (Virginia) Battery

Moody's (Louisiana) Battery

Parker's (Virginia) Battery

Taylor's (Virginia) Battery

Woolfolk's (Virginia) Battery

Reserve Artillery
MAJ. FELIX H. ROBERTSON

Barret's (Missouri) Battery, Capt. Overton W. Barret

LeGardeur's (Louisiana) Battery,[33] Capt. G. LeGardeur, Jr.

Havis' (Georgia) Battery, Capt. M.W. Havis

Lumsden's (Alabama) Battery, Capt. Charles L. Lumsden

Massenburg's (Georgia) Battery, Capt. T.L. Massenburg

CAVALRY[34]
MAJ. GEN. JOSEPH WHEELER

WHARTON'S DIVISION
BRIG. GEN. JOHN A. WHARTON

First Brigade
COL. C.C. CREWS

Malone's (Alabama) Regiment, Col. J.C. Malone, Jr.

2d Georgia, Lieut. Col. F.M. Ison

3d Georgia, Col. R. Thompson

4th Georgia, Col. Isaac W. Avery

Second Brigade
COL. THOMAS HARRISON

3d Confederate, Col. W.N. Estes

3d Kentucky, Lieut. Col. J.W. Griffith

4th Tennessee, Lieut. Col. Paul F. Anderson

8th Texas, Lieut. Col. Gustave Cook

11th Texas, Col. G.R. Reeves

White's (Tennessee) Battery, Capt. B.F. White, Jr.

---

[32] Did not arrive in time to take part in the battle. Jenkins' brigade assigned to the division September 11, 1863.

[33] Not mentioned in the reports, but in Reserve Artillery August 31, and Captain LeGardeur, etc., relieved from duty in Army of Tennessee November 1, 1863.

[34] From return of August 31, 1863, and reports.

MARTIN'S DIVISION
BRIG. GEN. WILLIAM T. MARTIN

First Brigade
COL. JOHN T. MORGAN
1st Alabama, Lieut. Col. D.T. Blakey
3d Alabama, Lieut. Col. T.H. Mauldin
51st Alabama, Lieut. Col. M.L. Kirkpatrick
8th Confederate, Lieut. Col. John S. Prather

Second Brigade
COL. A.A. RUSSELL
4th Alabama (Russell's Regiment), Lieut. Col. J.M. Hambrick
1st Confederate, Capt. C.H. Conner
J.H. Wiggins' (Arkansas) Battery, Lieut. J.P. Bryant

FORREST'S CORPS
BRIG. GEN. NATHAN B. FORREST

ESCORT
Jackson's Company Tennessee Cavalry, Capt. J.C. Jackson

ARMSTRONG'S DIVISION[35]
BRIG. GEN. FRANK C. ARMSTRONG

Armstrong's Brigade
COL. JAMES T. WHEELER
3d Arkansas, Col. A.W. Hobson
2d Kentucky, Lieut. Col. Thomas G. Woodward
6th Tennessee, Lieut. Col. James H. Lewis
18th Tennessee Battalion, Maj. Charles McDonald

Forrest's Brigade
COL. GEORGE G. DIBRELL
4th Tennessee, Col. William S. McLemore
8th Tennessee, Capt. Hamilton McGinnis
9th Tennessee, Col. Jacob B. Biffle
10th Tennessee, Col. Nicholas Nickleby Cox
11th Tennessee, Col. Daniel Wilson Holman
Shaw's Battalion, O.P. Hamilton's Battalion, and R.D. Allison's

[35] From return for August 31, 1863, and reports.

Squadron (consolidated), Maj. Joseph Shaw
Huggins' (Tennessee) Battery (formerly Freeman's),
Capt. A.L. Huggins.
Morton's (Tennessee) Battery, Capt. John W. Morton, Jr.

PEGRAM'S DIVISION[36]
BRIG. GEN. JOHN PEGRAM

Davidson's Brigade
BRIG. GEN. H.B. DAVIDSON
1st Georgia, Col. J.J. Morrison
6th Georgia, Col. John R. Hart
6th North Carolina, Col. George N. Folk
Rucker's (1st Tennessee) Legion, Col. E.W. Rucker (12th Tennessee
Battalion, Maj. G.W. Day, and 16th Tennessee Battalion,
Capt. John Q. Arnold[37])
Huwald's (Tennessee) Battery, Capt. Gustave A. Huwald

Scott's Brigade
COL. JOHN S. SCOTT
10th Confederate, Col. C.T. Goode
Detachment of John H. Morgan's command, Lieut. Col. R.M. Martin
1st Louisiana, Lieut. Col. James O. Nixon
2d Tennessee, Col. H.M. Ashby
5th Tennessee, Col. George W. McKenzie
N.T.N. Robinson's (Louisiana) Battery (one section),
Lieut. Winslow Robinson

ORGANIZATION OF
THE TROOPS IN EAST TENNESSEE
COMMANDER
LIEUT. GEN. JAMES LONGSTREET

McLAWS' DIVISION
MAJ. GEN. LAFAYETTE McLAWS

Kershaw's Brigade
2d South Carolina, Col. John D. Kennedy
3d South Carolina, Col. James D. Nance
7th South Carolina, Col. D. Wyatt Aiken

---

[36] Taken from Pegram's and Scott's reports and assignments, but the composition of the division is uncertain.
[37] Captain Company B, 12th Battalion

8th South Carolina, Col. John W. Henagan
15th South Carolina, Col. Joseph F. Gist
3d South Carolina Battalion, Lieut. Col. William G. Rice

Wofford's Brigade
16th Georgia, Col. Henry P. Thomas
18th Georgia, Col. S.Z. Ruff
24th Georgia, Lieut. Col. Luther J. Glenn
Phillips Legion, Lieut. Col. E.S. Barclay
3d Georgia Battalion Sharpshooters, Lieut. Col. N.L. Hutchins, Jr.

Humphreys' Brigade
13th Mississippi, Col. Kennon McElroy
17th Mississippi, Col. William D. Holder
18th Mississippi, Col. Thomas M. Griffin
21st Mississippi, Col. William L. Brandon

Bryan's Brigade
10th Georgia, Col. John B. Weems
50th Georgia, Col. Peter McGlashan
51st Georgia, Col. Edward Ball
53d Georgia, Col. James P. Simms

Artillery
MAJ. A. LEYDEN
Peeples' (Georgia) Battery, Capt. Tyler M. Peeples
Wolihin's (Georgia) Battery, Capt. Andrew M. Wolihin
York's (Georgia) Battery, Capt. Billington W. York

HOOD'S DIVISION
BRIG. GEN. MICAH JENKINS

Jenkins' Brigade
1st South Carolina, Col. Franklin W. Kilpatrick
2d South Carolina Rifles, Col. Thomas Thomson
5th South Carolina, Col. A. Coward
6th South Carolina, Col. John Bratton
Hampton Legion, Col. Martin W. Gary
Palmetto Sharpshooters, Col. Joseph Walker

Law's Brigade

4th Alabama, Col. Pinckney D. Bowles
15th Alabama, Col. William C. Oates
44th Alabama, Col. William F. Perry
47th Alabama, Col. M.J. Bulger
48th Alabama, Col. James L. Sheffield

Robertson's Brigade

3d Arkansas, Col. Van H. Manning
1st Texas, Col. A.T. Rainey
4th Texas, Col. J.C.G. Key
5th Texas, Col. R.M. Powell

Anderson's Brigade

7th Georgia, Col. W.W. White
8th Georgia, Col. John R. Towers
9th Georgia, Col. Benjamin Beck
11th Georgia, Col. F.H. Little
59th Georgia, Col. Jack Brown

Benning's Brigade

2d Georgia, Col. Edgar M. Butt
15th Georgia, Col. Dudley M. DuBose
17th Georgia, Col. Wesley C. Hodges
20th Georgia, Col. J.D. Waddell

Artillery

Col. E. Porter Alexander
Fickling's (South Carolina) Battery, Capt. William W. Fickling
Jordan's (Virginia) Battery, Capt. Tyler C. Jordan
Moody's (Louisiana) Battery, Capt. George V. Moody
Parker's (Virginia) Battery, Capt. William W. Parker
Taylor's (Virginia) Battery, Capt. Osmond B. Taylor
Woolfolk's (Virginia) Battery, Capt. Pichegru Woolfolk, Jr.

BUCKNER'S DIVISION[38]

BRIG. GEN. BUSHROD R. JOHNSON

Johnson's Brigade

17th and 23d Tennessee, Lieut. Col. Watt W. Floyd

25th and 44th Tennessee, Lieut. Col. John L. McEwen, Jr.

63d Tennessee, Maj. John A. Aiken

Gracie's Brigade1

41st Alabama, Lieut. Col. Theodore G. Trimmier

43rd Alabama, Col. Young M. Moody

1st Battalion, Hilliard's Alabama Legion, Maj. Daniel S. Troy

2d Battalion, Hilliard's Alabama Legion,

Lieut. Col. John W.A. Sanford

4th Battalion, Hilliard's Alabama Legion, Maj. John D. McLennan

CAVALRY CORPS

MAJ. GEN. WILLIAM T. MARTIN

MARTIN'S DIVISION

First Brigade

BRIG. GEN. JOHN T. MORGAN

1st Alabama, Lieut. Col. D.T. Blakey

3d Alabama, Lieut. Col. T.H. Mauldin

4th Alabama, Lieut. Col. J.M. Hambrick

7th Alabama, Col. James C. Malone, Jr.

51st Alabama, Capt. M.L. Kirkpatrick

Second Brigade

COL. J.J. MORRISON

1st Georgia, Lieut. Col. S.W. Davitte

2d Georgia, Lieut. Col. F.M. Ison

3d Georgia, Lieut. Col. R. Thompson

4th Georgia, Col. Isaac W. Avery

6th Georgia, Col. John R. Hart

[38] Attached to Longstreet's Corps.

ARMSTRONG'S DIVISION
BRIG. GEN. FRANK C. ARMSTRONG

First Brigade
BRIG. GEN. WILLIAM Y.C. HUMMS
4th Tennessee, Lieut. Col. Paul F. Anderson
8th Tennessee, Lieut. Col. Ferdinand H. Daugherty
9th Tennessee, Col. Jacob B. Biffle
10th Tennessee, Col. Nicholas N. Cox

Second Brigade
COL. C.H. TYLER
Clay's (Kentucky) Battalion, Lieut. Col. Ezekiel F. Clay
Edmundson's (Virginia) Battalion, Maj. Sylvester P. McConnell
Jessee's (Kentucky) Battalion, Maj. A.L. McAfee
Johnson's (Kentucky) Battalion, Maj. O.S. Tenney

WHARTON'S DIVISION

First Brigade
COL. THOMAS HARRISON
3d Arkansas, Lieut. Col. M.J. Henderson
65th North Carolina (Sixth Cavalry), Col. George N. Folk
8th Texas, Lieut. Col. Gustave Cook
11th Texas, Lieut. Col. J.M. Bounds

Artillery
Freeman's (Tennessee) Battery, Capt. A.L. Huggins
White's (Tennessee) Battery, Capt. B.F. White, Jr.
Wiggins' (Arkansas) Battery, Capt. J.H. Wiggins

RANSOM'S DIVISION
MAJ. GEN. ROBERT RANSOM, JR.

Corse's Brigade
BRIG. GEN. MONTGOMERY D. CORSE
15th Virginia, Lieut. Col. E.M. Morrison
29th Virginia, Col. James Giles
30th Virginia, Lieut. Col. Robert S. Chew

Wharton's Brigade Sharpshooters
BRIG. GEN. GABRIEL C. WHARTON
30th Virginia Battalion, Lieut. Col. J. Lyle Clarke
45th Virginia, Col. William H. Browne
51st Virginia, Col. Augustus Forsberg

Jackson's Brigade
BRIG. GEN. ALFRED E. JACKSON
Thomas' (North Carolina) Regiment, Lieut. Col. James R. Love
Walker's Battalion, Maj. James A. McKamy

Jones' Cavalry Brigade
BRIG. GEN. WILLIAM E. JONES
8th Virginia, Col. James M. Corns
21st Virginia, Col. William E. Peters
27th Virginia Battalion, Lieut. Col. Henry A. Edmundson[39]
34th Virginia Battalion, Lieut. Col. V.A. Witcher
36th Virginia Battalion, Capt. C.T. Smith
37th Virginia Battalion, Maj. James R. Claiborne

Williams' Cavalry Brigade
COL. H.L. GILTNER
16th Georgia Battalion, Maj. Edward Y. Clark
4th Kentucky, Maj. Nathan Parker
May's (Kentucky) Regiment, Lieut. Col. Edwin Trimble
1st Tennessee, Lieut. Col. Onslow Bean
64th Virginia, Col. Campbell Slemp

Jenkins' Cavalry Brigade
COL. MILTON J. FERGUSON
14th Virginia, Col. James Cochran
16th Virginia, Col. Milton J. Ferguson
17 Virginia, Maj. Frederick F. Smith

Artillery
Otey (Virginia) Battery, Capt. David N. Walker
Rhett (Tennessee) Battery, Capt. William H. Burroughs
Ringgold (Virginia) Battery, Capt. Crispin Dickenson
Tennessee Battery, Capt. Hugh L.W. McClung
Virginia Battery, Capt. George S. Davidson
Virginia Battery, Capt. William M. Lowry

[39] See Also Tyuler's brigade, Armstrong's division

FURTHER READING

Alexander, Edward Porter. *Fighting for the Confederacy: The Personal Recollections of General Edward Porter Alexander.* Edited by Gary W. Gallagher. Chapel Hill and London: University of North Carolina Press, 1989.

_____. *Military Memoirs of a Confederate.* Reprint. Bloomington: Indiana University Press, 1962.

Bridges, Hal. *Lee's Maverick General: Daniel Harvey Hill.* New York: McGraw Hill, 1961.

Buck, Irving. *Cleburne and His Command.* Reprint. Morningside Bookshop, 1982.

Connelly, Thomas L. *Army of the Heartland: The Army of Tennessee, 1861–1862.* Baton Rouge and London: Louisiana State University Press, 1967.

_____. *Autumn of Glory: The Army of Tennessee, 1862–1865.* Baton Rouge and London: Louisiana State University Press, 1971.

Connelly, Thomas, and Archer Jones. *The Politics of Command: Factions and Ideas in Confederate Strategy.* Baton Rouge and London: Louisiana State University Press, 1973.

Cozzens, Peter. *The Shipwreck of Their Hopes: The Battles For Chattanooga.* Urbana and Chicago: University of Illinois Press, 1994.

_____. *This Terrible Sound: The Battle of Chickamauga.* Urbana and Chicago: University of Illinois Press, 1992.

Eckenrode, H.J., and Bryan Conrad. *James Longstreet: Lee's War Horse.* Reprint. Chapel Hill and London: University of North Carolina Press, 1986.

Freeman, Douglas Southall. *Lee's Lieutenants: A Study in Command.* 3 vols. New York: Charles Scribner's Sons, 1942–44.

Hallock, Judith Lee. *Braxton Bragg and Confederate Defeat, Vol. II.* Tuscaloosa and London: University of Alabama Press, 1991.

Johnson, Robert Underwood, and Clarence Clough Buel, eds. *Battles and Leaders of the Civil War.* Reprint. 4 vols. New

York: Thomas Yoseloff, Inc., 1956. Volume 3 includes the events in this publication.

Lamers, William M. *The Edge of Glory: A Biography of General William S. Rosecrans, U.S.A.* New York: Harcourt, Brace, and World, 1961.

Lidell, St. John Richardson. *Liddell's Record.* Edited by Nathaniel C. Hughes. Dayton, Ohio: Morningside Bookshop, 1985.

Longstreet, James. *From Manassas to Appomattox: Memoirs of the Civil War in America.* Edited by James I. Robertson, Jr. New ed. Bloomington: Indiana University Press, 1960.

Manigault, Arthur Middleton. *A Carolinian Goes to War: The Civil War Narrative of Arthur Middleton Manigault.* Edited by R. Lockwood Tower. Columbia: University of South Carolina Press, 1983.

McDonough, James Lee. *Chattanooga—A Death Grip on the Confederacy.* Knoxville: University of Tennessee Press, 1984.

McKinney, Francis F. *Education in Violence: The Life of George H. Thomas and the History of the Army of the Cumberland.* Detroit, Michigan: Wayne State University Press, 1961.

McWhiney, Grady. *Braxton Bragg and Confederate Defeat, Vol. I.* Tuscaloosa and London: University of Alabama Press, 1969/1991.

McWhiney, Grady, and Perry Jamieson. *Attack and Die: Civil War Military Tactics and the Southern Heritage.* University: University of Alabama Press, 1982.

Parks, Joseph H. *General Leonidas Polk, C.S.A., The Fighting Bishop.* Baton Rouge and London: Louisiana State University Press, 1962.

Piston, William Garrett. *Lee's Tarnished Lieutenant: James Longstreet and His Place in Southern History.* Athens and London: University of Georgia Press, 1987.

Sanger, Donald Bridgman, and Thomas Robson Hay. *James Longstreet.* Baton Rouge and London: Louisiana State University Press, 1952.

Sorrel, G. Moxley. *Recollections of a Confederate Staff Officer.* Reprint. Dayton, Ohio: Morningside Bookshop, 1978.

Tucker, Glenn. *Chickamauga: Bloody Battle in the West.*
Reprint. Dayton, Ohio: Morningside Bookshop, 1984
Wert, Jeffry D. *General James Longstreet: The Confederacy's
Most Controversial Soldier—A Biography.* New York: Simon
& Schuster, 1993.

PHOTO CREDITS

We gratefully acknowledge the assistance of the Library of
Congress for the photographs of E.P. Alexander, Braxton
Bragg, Simon Bolivar Buckner, Ambrose E. Burnside, Patrick
R. Cleburne, Ulysses S. Grant, Micah Jenkins, Robert E. Lee,
James Longstreet, William W. Mackall, Arthur M. Manigault,
William Preston, James A. Seddon, G. Moxley Sorrel, George
H. Thomas, and Louis T. Wigfall.

We appreciate the cooperation of the U.S. Army Military
History Institute at Carlisle Barracks, Pennsylvania for the
photographs of Jefferson Davis, D.H. Hill, Evander McIvor
Law, Lafayette McLaws, and Leonidas Polk.

The photograph of the title page of a version of Mary
Chesnut's diary is taken from *A Diary from Dixie,* edited by
Isabella D. Martin and Myrta Lockett Avary (Peter Smith,
Gloucester, Mass., 1961).

INDEX

Alexander, Edward Porter, 66–67, 68, 77–78, 80

Anaconda Plan, 13

Anderson, Richard H., 60, 65

Appomattox Court House, Va, 18, 58, 67

Army of Northern Virginia, 23

Army of Tennessee, 14, 15, 17, 21, 24, 28, 32, 40, 41, 43, 44,
    45, 46, 47, 48, 50, 52, 53, 69

Atlanta Campaign, 28, 32, 46

Avary, Myra Lockett, 83

Beauregard, Gustave Toutant, 20, 32, 43, 51, 52, 66

Bentonville, NC, 43, 63

Bishop, Mary Richmond, 70

Black Hawk War, 19

Bowling Green, KY, 44, 46, 47

Bragg, Braxton, 14, 15, 16, 19, 20–21, 25, 27, 28, 36, 37, 38,
    41, 41, 42, 43, 44, 45, 46, 47, 48, 50, 51, 52–53, 54,
    56, 57, 58, 60–61, 65, 66, 69, 71, 80, 82, 84

Bratton, John, 61

Breckinridge, John C., 47, 61

Brent, George, 71

Bridgeport, AL, 57, 63

Brooks, Preston, 50

Brotherton House, 27

Brown, John, 23

Brown's Ferry, 57

Bruce, Sarah, 52

Buchanan, James, 47, 52

Buckner, Simon Bolivar, 41, 44, 71

Buell, D.C., 21

Burnside, Ambrose E., 69, 70, 73, 75, 80

Calhoun, John C., 52

Callaway, Dulcinea, 32
Callaway, Joshua K., 31–36
Campbell's Station, TN, 73
Catoosa Station, GA, 17, 25
Chaffin's Bluff, 67
Chancellorsville, VA, 18, 49, 67
Chattanooga, TN, 14, 15, 21, 28, 30, 32, 36, 40, 54, 57, 58,
    67, 68, 69, 71, 80, 84
Cheat Mountain, 23
Chesnut, James, Jr., 43, 82
Chesnut, Mary Boykin, 53, 81, 82–83
Chickamauga, 15, 18, 19, 21, 25–37, 38, 41, 43, 45, 46, 47,
    48, 57, 60, 62, 68, 84
Cleburne, Patrick, 41, 46
Cold Harbor, VA, 58, 63, 67
Connelly, Thomas, 67
Corinth, MS, 47, 56
Cracker Line, 54, 84
Cross, Charlotte, 50
Custis, Mary Ann Randolph, 22

Davis, Jefferson, 16, 19, 21, 23, 28, 41, 43, 44, 45, 46, 48, 49,
    51, 52, 53, 66–67, 69, 71, 82
Davis, Varina Howell, 19, 82
Department of Virginia and North Carolina, 20–21
Drewry's Bluff, 67

Ellis, Eliza Brooks, 20
Elzey, Arnold, 60
Emmitsburg Road, 22

Fairfax, John W., 50
First Manassas (or Bull Run), VA, 18, 60, 62, 65, 66, 70
Floyd, J.B., 45
Fort Donelson, 45, 58

Fort Fisher, 21
Fort Hamilton, 22
Fort Monroe, 19, 22
Fort Pulaski, 22, 65
Fort Sanders, 78–80
Fort Sumter, 32, 82
Franklin, TN, 32, 46
Fredericksburg, VA, 18, 49, 60, 62, 67, 70
Freeman, Douglas Southall, 49

Garland, Maria Louisa, 18
Geary, John W., 61
Gettysburg, PA, 13, 18, 20, 21–23, 24, 49, 62, 67
Grant, Ulysses S., 13, 18, 21, 45, 57, 58, 69, 70
Grigsby, Warren, 63

Hardee, William J., 46, 56
Harper's Ferry, VA, 23
Hatcher's Run, 65
Hill, Daniel Harvey, 41, 42, 60
Hindman, Thomas C., 15, 41
Hood, John Bell, 27–28, 32, 45, 48, 56, 57, 60, 62–63
Hopkins, Francis M., 34
Houston, Sam, 50
Howard, Oliver Otis, 62
Hunter, David, 43
Hunter, Robert M.T., 52

Island Number 10, 48

Jackson, Thomas J. "Stonewall", 49
Jameson, Caroline, 60
Jenkins, Micah, 60, 61, 62, 63, 66, 75, 78
Johnston, Albert Sidney, 20, 47, 48, 56
Johnston, Joseph E., 21, 23, 28, 42, 43, 48, 49, 51, 52, 60, 66

Kentucky Campaign, 14, 20–21, 28, 46, 56

Knoxville, TN, 18, 49, 60, 67, 69, 70, 71–80, 81, 83, 84

Latta, Jane Elizabeth, 62

Law, Evander McIvor, 60, 61, 62–63, 73, 75

Lee, Robert E., 13, 18, 20, 22–23, 24, 42, 46, 47, 48, 49, 56, 65, 67, 83

Liddell, St. John Richardson, 52–53, 58, 71

Lincoln, Abraham, 44, 52, 70

Little Round Top, 22

Longstreet, James, 16, 17–24, 25, 27, 30, 31, 32, 36–37, 38, 40, 41, 42, 43–52, 53, 54, 56, 57, 58, 60, 61, 62, 63–68, 69, 70, 71, 73, 75, 76–77, 78, 79, 80, 81–84

Lookout Mountain, 40, 54, 56, 57–58

Loudon, TN, 71

McLaws, Lafayette, 42, 45, 49, 62–63, 79, 81, 82, 84

McLemore's Cove, 15, 25, 41

Mackall, William Whann, 42, 48, 65

Mahone, William, 65

Manigault, Arthur M., 31, 32, 84

Marietta, GA, 28, 41

Martin, Isabella, 83

Mason, James M., 50

Meade, George, 58, 70

Mexican War, 18, 19, 20, 22, 32, 42, 44, 47, 48, 49, 56, 58, 70

Middle Tennessee, 14

Missionary Ridge, 40, 46, 57

Mobile, AL, 20, 21

Montgomery, AL, 82

Murfreesboro, TN, 14, 21, 28, 32, 46, 47

Nashville, TN, 14, 57

New Madrid, 48

New Orleans, LA, 18, 19, 45

Noll House, 40

North Anna River, VA, 63

Pendleton, William Nelson, 66
Peninsular Campaign, 18, 60, 66
Pensacola, FL, 20
Petersburg, VA 58, 65, 67, 70
Pickett, George E., 60
Pickett's Charge, 23, 67
Pierce, Franklin, 19
Pillow, G.J., 45
Polk, Leonidas, 15, 25, 27, 28, 36, 37, 40, 41, 53
Preston, William, 41, 47

Racoon Mountain, 58
Reed's Bridge, 37
Reid, John C., 34
Rhett, Robert Barnwell, Sr., 52
Richmond, VA, 16, 18, 21, 53, 67, 73
Roosevelt, Theodore, 23
Rosecrans, William S., 14, 15, 18, 21, 40, 56–57
Russellville, TN, 83

Salem Church, 49
Scott, Winfield, 22, 44, 49
Second Menassas (or Bull Run), VA, 18, 43, 60, 62, 66
Seddon, James A., 41, 50, 51, 52–53
Seminole War, 20, 48, 50, 56
Seven Days' Battle, Va, 42, 60, 62, 66
Seven Pines Battle, VA, 42, 60, 62
Sharpsburg (or Antietam), MD., 18, 43, 49, 62, 66, 70
Shellmound, TN, 63
Sherman, W.T., 21, 49, 57
Shiloh, TN, 20, 28, 46, 47, 56, 58
Smith, E. Kirby, 21 45, 56
Smith, J.R., 35–36
Snodgrass Hill, 28, 30, 34
Sorrel, G. Moxley, 65, 68

Spotsylvania, VA, 58, 63
Stone's River, TN 57
Stoneman, George, 56
Taylor, Zachary, 19, 49
Thedford's Ford, 37
Thomas, George H., 28–30, 56–57
Tullahoma, TN, 14, 21
Tyler, John, 53

U. S. Military Academy, 17, 18, 19, 20, 22–23, 28, 42, 44, 48, 49, 56, 58, 66, 70
University of the South, TN, 28
Utah Expedition, 66

Van Dorn, Earl, 56
Vance, Zebulon B., 21
Vicksburg, 13, 58

Washington, D.C., 22, 56, 82
Washington and Lee University, 23
Wauhatchie, 60, 61–68, 84
Wheeler, Joseph, 71
Wigfall, Louis T., 46, 48, 50
Wilderness, VA 18, 58, 60, 63, 65, 70
Williamsburg, VA, 42
Winthrop, Stephen, 78